# Knee Deep in the Funk

# Knee Deep in the Funk

## Understanding the Connection Between Spirituality and Music

Tzvi Gluckin

Copyright © 2011 by Tzvi Gluckin

All rights reserved. No part of the material protected by this copyright notice may be reproduced or utilized in any form, electronic or mechanical, including photocopying, recording, or by any information storage and retrieval system, without written permission from the copyright owner.

ISBN-13: 978-0-9845856-1-8

Mekabel Press
100 Hano Street, Suite 28
Allston, MA 02134

Typesetting and Layout – Esther Zaretsky
Cover Design – Shira Greenberg www.shiragreenberg.com
Cover Photo – Kevin Unger
www.gluckin.com

Printed in the United States of America
15 14 13 12 11        10 9 8 7 6 5 4 3 2 1

"Even though I use a couple of dirty words,
I still believe in God."

— Charles Mingus[1]

# Table of Contents

Introduction – 1

1: LVS (Lead Vocalist Syndrome) – 5

2: Spirituality is a Relationship – 19

3: Our Bodies, Our Shoes – 31

4: Music and Drugs – 47

5: Music and Intuition – 59

6: Unity – 67

7: Sex – 77

8: Everybody Prays – 87

9: The Bull, the Horns, and Something to Grab – 97

10: Music as a Universal Language – 103

Endnotes – 111

# Introduction

Music is spiritual. Many people believe that. It seems obvious and intuitive. Most religions use music as an integral part of worship. Music is an essential aspect of meditation and prayer.

Music is a part of informal worship as well. You probably closed your eyes at a concert, in a club, sitting around a campfire, or falling asleep with your headphones and felt something. Music does something to you. That something is spiritual.

But few people can explain what that something is.

Musicians try and usually fail. They lack a definition of spirituality or a vocabulary to express their feelings. They talk about color, sunsets, energy, and universal love. Those are nice ideas, but they don't mean much. And they don't articulate the spiritual dimension in music – at least not in a way that makes sense.

Mystics, the clergy, gurus, and other spiritual types recognize a mystical dimension in music as well. But they also lack a way to explain it. They understand spirituality, but they don't know much about music. They make assumptions and generalizations that sound good but don't work. And most musicians can spot their mistakes and flimsy logic.

That confusion is the reason I wrote this book.

My goal is to discuss the connection between spirituality and music. Most people assume a connection exists and I hope to explain that in a way that makes sense. I will define my terms. I will speak clearly. And I will be honest. You will get a practical and working definition of spirituality. Hopefully it will be something you can use and apply. And hopefully it will be meaningful even if you struggle with big concepts like God and religion.

Spirituality is bigger than most people think it is. It isn't just about religion, prayer, meditation, and God. Spirituality – especially as it relates to music – is also about growth, relationships, drugs, and sex. I will discuss those things, too.

What else do you need to know?

I won't make moral pronouncements about music. I won't favor one style over another. All music is spiritual – at least it has the potential to be. Musical taste is subjective and based on many factors. Does satanic music exist? Do the planetary orbits play a song? Is one style more conducive to spirituality than others? I don't know. You may think so. You may disagree. And that is cool. Think about it and decide for yourself.

I talk a lot about my experiences with music and most of my examples are from rock and jazz. That is the music I listen to. I am sorry if that bothers you. I don't get off on classical music (unless it is something wild like Penderecki's *Threnody for the Victims of Hiroshima*). If my examples don't do it for you, replace them with Brahms, Donna Summer, Air Supply, John Cage, King Sunny Adé, Lady Gaga, Men at Work, Glenn Miller, Natalie Merchant, Lipa Schmeltzer, or whatever floats your boat. It doesn't matter. The message is important, not the style.

This is not a science book either. It doesn't quote many

studies. It isn't peer-reviewed. And it isn't out to prove anything. I did my best to make sure my facts are correct. And the science I discuss – especially in chapter ten – is accurate.

But don't miss the point.

I am a musician. I am a rabbi. I have a thick resume in both fields. I based this book on years of experience. I also based it on years of study, practice, performance, analysis of ancient texts, discussions with master musicians, studies with mystical masters, formal studies in both disciplines, and informal discussions with anyone who would listen. I discuss my experiences and explain my conclusions. I think it works. I think you will get something out of it.

And I tried to be practical. Music is an opportunity. I give tools, examples, and suggestions. Try them out. Understand what music is, what it does, how it is spiritual, and experience something special. And hopefully – and this is the point – you will use music to be happier, have better relationships, feel better about yourself, and appreciate other people.

Music is a tool. Use it to transcend. Use it to find God. And use it to be happy. Read the book, think about it, check it out, and decide for yourself.

# 1

# LVS
# (Lead Vocalist Syndrome)

The power of singing, background music, spirituality, relationships, and my friends the Beatles[2]

I have a degree in music. It took four years. I earned my BM – a Bachelors of Music – and my major was in Jazz Studies.

Music school was nerdy. No frats, parties, drugs, cheerleaders, or football. It wasn't like the high school in *Fame* either – no tubas in the bathroom. You practiced, worked hard, and that was about it. And music students – like most people – had inside jokes. Music students found them funny, nobody else did.

Here was one:

What do you call a person who hangs out with musicians?

A singer.

Hahaha.

Singers were usually offended because singing is hard work. Singers train for years learning how to breathe, how to hear, and how to nail a pitch. Doing it right, well, and consistently is a major accomplishment.

But that doesn't mean that other musicians can't make fun of them. Of course they can.

If a singer wasn't around, we changed the punch line. We replaced the word "singer" with "drummer." Not as funny, but it annoyed the drummer. And we had special drummer jokes, too. I liked this one: How do you know when a drummer is knocking at your door?

The knock gets faster.

Hahaha.

(Get it? Drummers are known to push the tempo when they get excited. We had jokes about guitarists and trombonists as well.)

But back to singers, why do other musicians make fun of them? Are they jealous?

I think they are. The singer gets the glory: he is the leader, he stands in front, he gets the girls, and he gets the most applause. The audience relates to the singer. The band – as far as the audience is concerned – is still just the band. They even refer to them as "backing musicians."

People enjoy listening to singers. They like music with vocals. Instrumental music is not as popular and you have to make an effort to appreciate it.

Instrumental music rarely makes the Top 40. Go back to when *Billboard Magazine* first started making charts. You won't find many instrumental hits. Instrumental music doesn't sell, at least not at the same level as music with vocals, and not enough to make the Top 40.

You will find exceptions. I remember "Hooked on Classics," a terrible hit from the early eighties. Louis Clark and the Royal Philharmonic recorded Beethoven,

Mozart, Rachmaninoff, and others over a four-on-the-floor disco beat. It was horrible. I don't know why it sold.

Chuck Mangione had a big hit with "Feels So Good," especially after it was featured at the 1980 Winter Olympics in Lake Placid, NY. "Frankenstein" by Edgar Winter was a number one hit in 1973. I am sure there are others, but not many. Instrumental music is a tough sell, especially when compared to vocal music.

Look at this quote from Frank Zappa:

> Apart from the snide political stuff, which I enjoy writing, the rest of [my] lyrics wouldn't exist at all if it weren't for the fact that we live in a society where instrumental music is irrelevant – so if a guy expects to earn a living by providing musical entertainment for folks in the U.S.A., he'd better figure out how to do *something* with a human voice plopped on it.[3]

It isn't that instrumental music isn't popular. It is popular. (And I disagree with Frank. It isn't irrelevant.) It sells. Plenty of people buy it. And many musicians have had long and successful careers playing it. It just isn't in the same league as music with vocals. Instrumental music is an acquired taste. And like anything that takes effort to appreciate, it has a limited audience.

In my mind, instrumental music is similar to single malt scotch. I don't understand single malt scotch. I think it tastes like paint thinner. But people who love it and appreciate it pay top dollar for a bottle of 75-year-old whatever. Instrumental music fans are the same. They spend a ton of money on it and they love it. You have to appreciate it, have exposure to it, and learn how to listen to it. But when you do, you get it.

Many people like music in the background as well. They call it "background music." Background music is almost always instrumental. It rarely features a singer.

I was visiting the dentist recently and he had solo piano music playing in the background. It played continuously. It was awful, but it is easy to tune out.

And the piano music was a subscription service. He paid for it. Why didn't he pay for something better? Why didn't he turn on the radio and play pop tunes?

He didn't do it, and he was content with the offensive piano drivel, because he didn't want to get distracted. If he were playing great tunes with words he could sing along with, he would focus on that. And he didn't want to focus on that. He wanted to focus on x-rays and drilling teeth.

Singing is distracting. It is hard to ignore.

Why is instrumental music less popular than music with vocals? Why is instrumental music an acquired taste like single malt scotch? Why is instrumental music a better choice as background music? What is distracting about singing?

Music is communication. It is a language. And the most powerful communication is direct. You can't beat face-to-face contact. "Look me in the eye." "Tell me to my face." You can't beat that. It is powerful. It is intense. The power is diminished when it is less direct. A phone call can be powerful. But it isn't the same as a live conversation. It loses something. Subtlety, nuance, these things get lost over the phone.

But a phone call still beats an email. At least you are talking. It is easy to misinterpret an email. You can't tell if the person is angry or sarcastic. You can't hear his tone of voice. And a text message – forget about it – piece together letters and symbols and hope for the best.

I was once giving a lecture to a group of college students. In the middle of it, a woman ran out of the room crying. "What did I do?" I thought. "What did I say?" Oh well. I continued my talk. I bumped into her in the hall after I finished. She was still crying.

"What happened? Why did you run out of my talk?" I asked her.

"Oh – sob – my boyfriend just broke up with me." She said.

"In the middle of my talk? How did you find out? Do you have special telepathic powers?"

"He texted me."

What?

My first thought was to give her a hard time for texting while I was speaking, but I decided against that. She was upset and that would be mean. My second reaction was probably the same as your reaction. I thought to myself, "What a jerk. Who dumps his girlfriend with a text message?"

When you are in a relationship, you talk, laugh, do things, and spend time together. Your feelings get stronger the longer you are together. Your partner means something to you. And if the relationship is over, it isn't like it never happened. You went through a lot together. You have to end it with dignity. You have to speak face-to-face. At least give her a call. It is wrong to end it with something impersonal and indirect like a text message.

I told her to never go out with him again, even if he groveled, begged, cried, or got down on his knees. Too bad and good-bye. He had a lot to learn. A relationship deserves real communication. Most people understand that.

I don't know if she listened to me.

What about the opposite – can you fall in love with a text message?

I was at a conference a few years ago. I met a psychiatrist. He was great. We had a lot in common and talked about our work. I talked about what I did. He told me about some of his clients. He had a lot of interesting clients.

One client appeared to be a normal guy. He had a job. He was presentable. He had been in relationships with women, but nothing ever worked out. And then he met the woman of his dreams. They had an amazing relationship. He never felt close to someone like he did with her. He never felt he could be as honest as he was with her. He never felt that someone understood him as well as she did. He was in love. He could just be himself. It was intense.

But they had never met in person. They never spoke on the phone. Never. They met online, sent text messages to each other, and that is as far as it got.

That is why someone sent him to a shrink. A relationship built exclusively on texting is weird. It is missing direct contact. Nothing actually happened. It is like falling in love with a character in a book. It is two-dimensional. You are not getting the full picture. You only see what the author wants you to see.

Odd huh?

Communication builds closeness. It creates intimacy. It creates a connection.

Think about it. You meet someone in a bar. You don't know each other. She looks good. He looks hot. Whatever. You can fantasize and think about this person all you want. It is wonderful. At least it seems wonderful in your head. But in real life, you don't know anything until you start talking.

But once you start talking you realize – quickly – that she is boring or he is a jerk. It doesn't take long. You can tell. You can feel it. And you are usually right.

Communication gets the ball rolling. You learn enough about someone in a quick conversation to know if you want to see him or her again. It is not enough communication to get married or fall madly in love, but a conversation – even a short one – is enough to sense that there is something worth building on.

And what happens on your next date? You talk some more. Through talking you get to know each other better. You bond. You feel closer. You can sense if there is more to this relationship and if you want to take it further. You can tell.

At some point it gets serious. Serious is scary. Serious means you know each other well. Serious is one step before the M word. Yikes.

Serious people like to talk to me. I am a rabbi. I am cool. I do it all. And serious people want to know one thing, "How do you know?"

I tell them that knowing is easy. You just need communication. If you are comfortable, if you can be yourself, if you can say what you mean, and if you are relaxed – you are ready to get married. It is that simple. No one is perfect. The perfect person doesn't exist. Everyone makes mistakes. Everyone has faults. And even perfect people change. But if you can communicate, you have the basis for a great relationship. Yes, there are other factors involved. Yes, there are other things to think about. But the other issues are secondary. Communication is king.

Some people say, "It is too comfortable." "We are best friends." "I feel like I am talking to my sister." Duh. Open and easy communication is not a negative. It is the sign of a great relationship. Go for it.

Apply this concept to music. Relationships are built on communication. Direct communication is the most powerful. And music is a language, a form of communication. When you listen to music, the musician is communicating with you.

Vocal music is the singer speaking to you – directly – his voice to your ear. There is no intermediary, tool, device, or anything. It is his voice. It is easy to connect to him. You hear his voice and it draws you in. You have a one-way conversation – he is talking and you are listening.

Instrumental music is different. It is indirect; the musician is speaking with his instrument. It takes effort to listen to. It is easy to tune it out or leave it in the background. It is like a phone call on a bad line, you have to make an effort to hear it. And that is why it is an acquired taste. If you aren't listening, you aren't going to appreciate it. It is harder to tune out a voice. It is like ignoring someone who is trying to tell you something.[4]

Don't misunderstand, instrumental music is popular and powerful, but it isn't for everyone. It isn't effortless. You have to listen to it to appreciate it. The experience isn't automatic.

And a great vocal performance is powerful. My wife was once watching a cheesy British version of American Idol. Next up was a Welsh guy. He wasn't cool. He was missing teeth. But then he started singing. My wife cried. She watched it again and cried again. I think she cries every time she watches it. (The video is on YouTube, she hits replay over and over again). That nerdy Welsh guy spoke straight to her heart. He got in. That is what a great voice can do.

Great guitar solos can move you as well, but it isn't the same. It isn't instant. It isn't easy. You have to pay attention.

And communication creates intimacy. Listen to someone speak – even a boring lecture – you feel like he is speaking to you.

Don't you?

It is weird – but think about it – it is true. It doesn't matter what he is talking about or how many people are in the audience. You feel like he is talking to you. You relate to him. You feel like you know him. You feel comfortable with him. You will talk to him after his lecture; ask him questions, shmooze, and you won't be intimidated. You might even share a personal story.

He spoke. He let you in. A wall separating you was broken. And he didn't do anything. He didn't introduce himself, shake your hand, or buy you a gift. He just spoke. But speaking is enough. Communication exposes one person to another and that exposure is relatable. It is the glue that connects people together.

Music – the language – works the same way, and listening is enough. Even a recording is enough.

I was turned on to the Beatles when I was about ten years old. It was the late Seventies. I was at summer camp and a kid in my bunk was a Beatles nut. He played their music constantly. I thought it was great and got hooked. I bought the red and blue greatest hits albums and wore out the grooves – I listened to them so much. My best friend gave me blank tapes and made me record my Beatles music for him. I did it. I didn't care. I was happy to spread the word. And the more I listened, the more I liked it. I bought more albums (and made more tapes for my friend), studied the pictures, read the liner notes, read articles, and filled my world with everything Beatles.

And – this is the point – I felt like I knew them. I discussed the Beatles with my friends. I used their first names. "I love George's solo on *The End*." "Paul is amazing on *Helter Skelter*." The Beatles were my friends. I felt connected. I was bummed when John was killed. I wasn't alone. Millions of people felt the same way.

And I was normal. Most of the other people who loved the Beatles were normal too. I understood that I didn't *actually* know them. I didn't need to see a psychiatrist. But being normal didn't prevent me from feeling close to them. They were a part of my world. I cared. They spoke to me. Their music spoke to me. And that conversation created intimacy. Communication creates intimacy. I felt connected. The Beatles and I were friends.

That is what music does. Music, like any language, brings people together. It creates intimacy. It connects people to each other. And the beauty of music is that the language is universal. It transcends boundaries like culture, generation, and spoken language.

And as powerful as it is to listen, it is even more powerful when you do the talking. A professional headhunter once told me the secret to a great job interview – i.e. how to get hired. Don't talk. Let the interviewer talk. Your great tie, resume, speaking skills, connections, and knowledge are secondary. The important thing is how the interviewer feels. If he likes you, you're in. If he doesn't, you're not. If you do all the talking, you are boring. If he does all the talking, he is excited. He likes how the interview felt (of course he did, he didn't stop talking) and he associates you with those good feelings. You can't lose.

When you go to a concert and the singer says, "I love you all," he really means it. No joke. You probably think, "Show biz celebrity moron." But that isn't fair. He is in the zone. He is lost in the high of performance. He just poured his heart out. He expressed himself and said something important. And you were the one he was talking to. He feels connected.

A performer bonds with his audience. That bond is the result of honest communication. Communication creates relationships. It happens on a date, in a bar, or on a stage. The connection is the result of sharing something in a language that the listener understands. The singer spoke to you with music. You feel a bond with him. He feels connected to you.

Think about the last time you sat around a campfire. You were with a group of people. Someone had a guitar. A few folksy old hippie types were there too. Someone sang. Others joined in. You joined in too, why not? And it was awesome. It was awesome in spite of the old hippies, cheesy songs, bugs, and burnt marshmallows. When it was over you wanted a hug. (Even awkward uncomfortable British people hug at campfires.) The hug was an expression of how you felt. You communicated in a common and understood language. And you felt connected.

That feeling is why music is a universal spiritual language. Spirituality is a relationship (I will explain why in the next section). Relationships are built on communication.

Music is a universal aspect of spirituality. Almost every religion, group, sect, tribe, cult, or mystical gathering involves music as part of its worship. It doesn't matter if the service is formal or informal. It doesn't matter if the service is in a synagogue, mosque, function hall, bonfire, circle in the woods, church, or standing in the guts of an elephant – music is central to the experience. The music could be serious, fun, meditative, contemplative, heavy, light, physical, ethereal, overwhelming, in the background, interactive, spontaneous, improvised, structured, or whatever. It doesn't matter. Whatever the music, it is still music, and it is an ever-present part of the spiritual experience.

Oliver Sacks, in his book *Musicophilia* (a book about music and the brain), quotes Aniruddh Patel at the Neurosciences Institute about the universality of music and notes that:

> "In every culture there is some form of music with a regular beat, a periodic pulse that affords temporal coordination between performers, and elicits synchronized motor response from listeners." This linking of auditory and motor systems seems universal in humans, and shows itself spontaneously, early in life.[5]

In my community – the Orthodox Jewish community – music is a communal and interactive part of worship. Someone usually leads the service, but the leader's role is pragmatic; he keeps the group together. Everyone is expected to sing and participate. Sometimes the mood is somber and intense. Other times it is joyous and you dance. It is interactive. It is similar to a campfire – except that you are inside and wearing clean clothes. And when you sing, you feel a connection.

That connection is spiritual. It is a connection with God, energy, a force, or whatever you want to call it. Music is the language. It is the same bond a singer feels with his audience. It is the same bond you feel at a campfire. And it doesn't matter if the conversation is one-way. Communicating is enough to feel a connection. The connection is strong. It is palpable. It is real and you feel it.

And it is powerful. It rubs off on the people around you. Look at this example of when it happened to me.

In the mid-nineties, I was a student at a yeshiva in Jerusalem. It was the end of the summer and time for the High Holidays. The most intense part of High Holiday preparation is reserving your seat. You want a good seat. Other people want your seat. It is a battle. You have to have connections and understand the system.

That year was my third or fourth year at the yeshiva. I had seniority. I knew how to get a good seat. And I wanted to sit in the back.

I found a seat in the back row, behind a big pole. It was perfect. I pulled a few strings and it worked. The seat was reserved in my name. I was set.

That year, the yeshiva started a Russian division. It was for students from the former Soviet Union. The Russian division was separate. It was in a separate building. It had separate classes. The students from the Russian program didn't mix with the students in my program. But for the High Holidays, the administration decided to combine the Russians with everyone else. And there was a Russian student who wanted my seat. His name was Moshe. He tried to pull strings, but it didn't work. He was too late and I had seniority. But they gave him the seat next to me. Not bad and a great seat for a new guy.

The Jewish High Holidays are three days over a tenday period. The first two days – Rosh Hashanah – are the Jewish New Year. The last day – ten days later – is Yom

Kippur, an intense day of fasting and prayer. The services start in the evening and continue for most of the next day. They are intense, serious, long, and almost entirely sung. It is easy to get lost in the experience.

Services started. I sat in my seat. Moshe showed up a few minutes late and took his seat next to me. We prayed. We sang. It was intense. We didn't talk. You don't talk during services. After Rosh Hashanah Moshe went back to the Russian division. I did my thing at the yeshiva.

Yom Kippur was a week later. We sat next to each other. Same thing. He showed up late. We didn't speak to each other. We sang. We prayed. And by the end of Yom Kippur, we were best friends.

Wow. How did that happen?

That is the power of music. We didn't speak to each other. But we did. Music brought us together. We communicated. We were open. We bypassed the informal getting-to-know-you stage and became friends. And it worked. It is more than fifteen years later and we are still friends.

Singing is talking. Music is language. Language is communication. And communication brings people together.

Music is a spiritual language if you want it to be. It is a conversation with God. The connection is up to you.

# 2
# Spirituality is a Relationship.

### The problem with Romeo and the emotional power of AC/DC

Relationships and spirituality share a common vocabulary.

Relationships are about connection, closeness, love, and intimacy. When you are apart, you feel a yearning and desire. When you are together you feel at one and united. Spirituality is similar. You feel connected and close. You feel love and intimacy. You experience unity and oneness. You long for it.

Relationships and spirituality use similar language, but are they built from the same stuff?

The backbone of a good relationship is communication. You cannot have a relationship if you cannot communicate. You can't get started. If you have nothing to talk about, no common ground, no understanding – you have nothing to work with.

Did you ever go on a bad date? A mutual friend suggested it. It looked good on paper. You had the same interests. You had similar views. You grew up in the same town. And then you met and it was as if he or she was raised in a parallel universe. The conversation was awkward and strained – it didn't flow. You had nothing to talk about. You couldn't understand each other. You couldn't be yourself. It was unnatural. And you wanted to leave. She was nice. He was ok. But it wasn't for you. You couldn't communicate.

But when it worked – wow – it clicked. Do you remember the first time you met your spouse, a good friend, or someone you like to talk to? And I don't mean the first time you saw each other, just the first time it worked – the first time you really talked. You knew. You met at work, on the train, in a store, in a bar, at a party, at school, or wherever it was. You talked. And you talked and you talked. It was like magic. You felt it. You had what to say. It flowed. You connected. And the content of your conversation was immaterial – maybe you liked the same things or maybe you disagreed about everything – it didn't matter. What mattered was that you communicated. You connected. And from that point on he or she was in your life.

I remember my second date with my wife. We were set up. Our first date was nice, but it wasn't incredible. A friend convinced my wife to go out with me again. And that was it. We talked for hours and hours. We laughed – we couldn't stop laughing – and we had a great time. We walked around. We got lost. We ended up in a parking lot. We found a chair in a dumpster and my wife made me carry it back to her apartment. It was a crazy night. We went on more dates, but I knew from that night that we were going to get married. We just hit it off.

And just like communication brings people together, a lack of communication pulls people apart.

At first something happened. Tension. Maybe you had a disagreement – that is normal. Maybe it was about something serious or maybe it was trivial. Whatever it was, you didn't deal with it and it festered. Festering is bad news. Festering means the problem still exists, but it is ignored. It isn't discussed. And worse, you stop talking. The longer you let it sit, the worse it gets. And it can get bad. A world of disagreements, problems, arguments, and assumptions multiply in your head. "That dirty rat." "I hope he dies." But the disagreements are only in your head. You don't discuss it.

But if you don't deal with it – like have a big fight or intense discussion – eventually you will hit a point of no return. And then it is too late. You have nothing more to talk about and the relationship is over.

Look at this quote from Ozzy Osbourne about the breakup of Black Sabbath:

> After all that time on the road, we'd just had enough of each other's company. But when we didn't spend any time together, all our problems grew in our heads, and we stopped communicating.[6]

The Black Sabbath story is typical. They were a great band. They grew up together. They became famous together. They toured for months without a break and when they weren't on tour they were in rehearsal, writing new music, or in the studio. They were inseparable. And then they stopped communicating and everything fell apart. Many great bands break up for the same reason.

Why is communication so important?

The Jewish mystics explain it like this. The Bible (Genesis 2:7) states that, "God blew into man a breath of life and he became a living being." What type of breath is blown from the mouth of God? It refers to man's rational soul, as evidenced by his ability to speak.[7] Speaking – or any communication – reveals your inner essence (or at least as much as you want to reveal).

Or say it another way; communication is magic. It reveals a secret world. It reveals your thoughts. It reveals you.

I am an inert blob with hair. You don't know me. You don't know anything about me. But when I communicate I come alive. It doesn't matter if I say something, sing a song, or twitch my nose. I do something, you get the point, and it breaks the ice. I let you in. I become someone. And you can relate to me.

And just like when I communicate you learn about me, when you communicate I learn about you. You are an inert blob, too. When you communicate you come alive. You become someone. You express yourself. You are yourself. I – the listener – have something to relate to. I relate to you. And this is the amazing part, not only do I feel closer, but you – the communicator – feel close to me as well. It is true even if I am not really listening. You feel a bond. Speaking is a powerful connecting agent for both the speaker and listener.

You experience this all the time. Do you have a pet? Do you love your pet? Why? Do you think your pet loves you? Do you think your pet knows what love is? You talk to your pet. You communicate. You look into his eyes. You rub his neck. You express yourself. And you feel connected. The feeling is strong. But what do you think the animal is thinking? He is probably thinking, "Food." "Kill." "Smell." I doubt he is thinking about you, love, closeness, unity, or the depth of your relationship.

But you are. You conjure up a wonderful world of love, companionship, and mutual affection. It is in your head. But it doesn't matter. You feel it. And it is because you communicated. So what if the communication was only one-way. You expressed yourself.

A one-way communication is enough to give a sense of connection. You feel something. And that is good. But the thing that makes communicating a relationship is when the other person reciprocates. A two-way conversation is more than a warm fuzzy feeling. A two-way conversation is real.

I felt a connection to the Beatles. Their music spoke to me. They were a part of my world. I was connected and it was a strong feeling. But I knew that I didn't really know them. If I thought I did it would have been weird. I would have been a deranged fan. A deranged fan cannot distinguish between his feelings and reality. He doesn't understand that the conversation is only one-way.

When the singer tells his audience, "I love you all," part of that is one-way. He communicated, sang his heart out, poured his guts out, and felt connected. But he also heard the audience's applause. He heard their outpouring of love and support. It is a powerful feeling. True, the relationship is superficial. He didn't have an intense one-on-one conversation with each person in the crowd. But it is a two-way connection nonetheless.

Your hippie campfire experience was a two-way conversation as well. You let your hair down. You connected to the other people. They connected to you. That was the reason for the group hug. The songfest was a reciprocal love-in. You felt it.

And a spiritual experience is based on the same principles. It is a conversation. You express yourself and feel a connection. And spirituality is mind-blowing. You know you aren't alone. You know the conversation isn't one-way. It is not like talking to your dog or to yourself. You don't feel stupid or self-conscious. Something happened. Could it be psychological? Could it be delusional? It could be. But I don't think it is. If you experienced it, you don't think it is either. You talked – however you did it; prayer, meditation, music, thoughts – and you were listened to. It was private. It was intimate. And you felt something.

Communication reveals an inner world – I mentioned that above – it reveals as much as you want to reveal. But there is more.

Pretend that we met for the first time. I said, "Hello." You said, "Hello." "What is your name?" "Francis." "Where are you from?" "Cleveland." "Do you like tomatoes?" "No." "Neither do I, I hate tomatoes." It was a typical first meeting. We gathered information. I don't know much about you and I don't know if we have much in common, except that we both hate tomatoes.

Most of your interactions never get much deeper. They are superficial and limited. You meet hundreds of people. You know who each person is. You recognize his face. You know his name. You interact with him regularly. And that is about it. The security guy at your office, the person who serves you coffee every morning, your mechanic, the dry cleaner, the crossing guard at your kid's school, the fat guy who lives two doors down and across the street – you see these people every day. But they aren't your friends. You won't be heartbroken when they leave town. You won't think about them when you leave town. They exist. They are a part of your world. You will replace them multiple times as you move, change jobs, get older, and get on with life. Your relationship with them isn't deep. It never gets beyond exchanging information. It is intellectual.

But many people mean more to you. Your relationship isn't superficial. You care about them.

Take work. You have people in your office, on your floor, in your division, clients, and customers, and you deal with them all the time. You know them. You know more than their names and where they come from. You know their mannerisms, quirks, and idiosyncrasies. You know what makes them mad. You know about their personal lives. You know their spouses and children. You know their politics. You know if they like football and what music they listen to. You interact with them constantly. You solve problems together. You joke around at boring meetings. You argue about parking, using the bathroom, paying for coffee, and petty things in the office. You forge alliances against the boss. You give them advice. You talk about personal problems. You get drunk with them at the company picnic and hang out on business trips.

And that type of interaction happens all the time. It happens at work, at school, on vacation, at family gatherings with distant cousins – any time you get together with people. You won't relate to everyone, and you won't talk to the people you don't relate to unless you have to. But you will connect with others. And when you connect, you talk and talk. You become kindred spirits, blood brothers, and partners in crime – you bond. You enjoy being together. You talk and interact – a lot – and get to know each other.

At some point your interaction stops being an intellectual exchange of ideas – What was your name again? Where are you from? – and you become friends. Your heart gets involved. You feel an emotional connection. You care. You know him and you know much about him. You know his strengths. You forgive his weaknesses.

You care about these people. You go to their family celebrations. You share in their accomplishments. You cry with them in hard times. You eulogize them when they die. Your relationship is no longer just intellectual. It is emotional.

This same process – just more intense – is how you meet your spouse. You meet. You talk. You date. You get to know each other. At some point it gets serious and you get married. The relationship is built on communication. Communication starts the process, keeps the ball rolling, and is at the heart of the relationship.

And the more you communicate, the deeper the relationship. You can't compare lovebird high school sophomores to forty years of marriage. They are different realities. If the high school couple breaks up, it is a bummer. It isn't a tragedy. They think it is, but please. *Romeo and Juliet* is a tragedy because Romeo and Juliet were idiots. They didn't know each other. They were self-absorbed, self-centered, immature teenagers. Compare Romeo and Juliet to a man who lost his wife of forty years. You can't. You can't compare a lifetime to a high school romance. Forty years is a lifetime of communication and interaction.

Closeness, understanding, and connection are the result of communication. The more you know, the more you relate to, the more you understand, and the closer you grow. Understanding creates an emotional bond. Even conflict – once it is resolved – brings you closer.

Communication opens the door to another person. It starts as a cold intellectual process. At some point you learn enough and it becomes emotional. Eventually it becomes intense. Look at the process: the inert blob becomes a person, the person becomes an acquaintance, the acquaintance becomes a friend, and the friend becomes a brother.

What about music?

Music is a shortcut. It is a language, but it is a different kind of language. It bypasses the intellect. It goes straight to the heart. It speaks to your emotions.

I was once driving on the Merritt Parkway in Connecticut. I was near New Haven. New Haven has a great classic rock station. You can only get it in central Connecticut. I listened to a few tunes and then they played *For Those About To Rock* by AC/DC. *For Those About To Rock* is a great song. It was released when I was in eighth grade. I never bought the album but I have always liked the song. I am happy when it is played on the radio. You can watch great concert footage of *For Those About To Rock* too.[8]

*For Those About To Rock* starts slow. It builds but it takes a while. It ends with a twenty-one-gun salute – AC/DC fire real cannons when they play it live – and the band kicks into double time. It is amazing.

The song came on the radio. I listened. I cranked it really loud. I sang along. It hit the double time part at the end. And I lost it. I cried my eyes out.

Picture the scene. It was insane. I was alone in my car, the music was blaring, and tears were streaming down my face. Imagine passing in a different car and looking over at me. Crazy. What's happening over there?

I don't know what happened – I don't know why it happened – but something happened. The song spoke to me. It triggered something weird in my subconscious and unleashed a tirade.

Odd? Yes. Unusual? Yes.

But normal.

That is what music does. Music bypasses your intellect and speaks to your emotions. It isn't rational. It doesn't make sense. But it happens. It happens all the time. It happened when my wife listened to the Welsh guy. It happened to me on the Merritt Parkway. I bet it had something to do with the insanity of Beatlemania in the early sixties. You can probably come up with a million examples.

Music speaks to your heart. It skips the dry intellectual exchange of information, "What is your name?" "Where are you from?" It gets straight to the point. You feel it at a concert. You experience it at a campfire. It relaxes you enough to hug a total stranger.

Look at this quote taken from the introduction to a study about the effects of music on memory:

Music has an amazing power to influence man's emotions and behavior. It has been found to affect and stimulate many different parts of the brain and body. Psychological study of music is based on this reason.[9] [10]

Music is an emotional language. It brings people together. It speaks in a way that isn't intellectual. Think about your favorite song. You probably don't know all the words. And it doesn't matter. The words are secondary. The important thing is the connection. The music speaks to you.

Spirituality is a relationship. Relationships are built on communication. Music is an emotional language; it skips the dry introductory exchange of information and gets straight to the point. It speaks to your heart. And that is why music is central to the spiritual experience. It is why almost every religion, group, sect, tribe, cult, or mystical gathering involves music as part of its worship. It is why most musicians think their music is spiritual as well.

Spirituality is a conversation and music is the most direct language. Music makes the conversation emotional. It creates connections. It speaks to the heart.

# 3

# Our Bodies, Our Shoes

### Your bad character is destroying your spirituality

I hate the beach. Some people love it, but I don't. I hate the heat, that sticky feeling, and sand in my shorts. And something always goes wrong whenever I go. I am sure you feel the same way.

Remember your last trip to the beach? You went. You took as little with you as possible – just a towel and suntan lotion (taking a little was a precaution because most beaches are crawling with criminals). You drove to the beach barefoot – no flip-flops – and wore just a bathing suit. When you got there, you parked a few cars from the sand.

And that was when the trouble started.

You were parked just a few cars from the beach. But a few cars might as well have been a few miles. The parking lot wasn't paved – it was hot, sharp gravel – not that pavement would have helped. And duh, you left your shoes at home – how did you think you were going to get from the car to the beach? Fly?

Walking to the beach is a no-brainer when you have shoes or flip-flops or sandals or flippers or whatever. You don't think about it. You do it. It isn't an issue.

But you drove to the beach barefoot. Genius.

You stepped out of the car. Ouch! Hot! Yikes. One step. Ouch. Next step. Help! You couldn't run – the parking lot was gravel – so you suffered. Five minutes felt like an hour. The pain was unbearable. You persevered and – finally – you made it. But your day was ruined because you couldn't stop thinking about the walk back to the car.

Do you take your shoes for granted? Most people do. You need shoes. You can't do much without them. Shoes give you mobility. They enable you to get around. They help you navigate the world. Try walking around New York City without shoes. Impossible. (And disgusting.)

People have always worn shoes. Shoes have been found on archeological digs from Oregon to Africa. They are painted on the walls of caves. The ancient Egyptians, Chinese, Israelites, Greeks, Romans, and others discussed them and attached significance to them.[11] Shoes are a ubiquitous feature of human history.

And shoes are essential to understanding spirituality. The shoe gives the foot mobility. It gives it life. And so too the body – spiritually speaking – is a shoe for the soul. The body gives the soul a place. It gives it a place to go, a way to function, and the means to get things done. A soul without a body is barefoot. It is useless.

Shoes and spirituality are all over the Bible. God told Moses to take off his shoes at the Burning Bush.[12] Shoes are the key to understanding the Levirate Marriage in Deuteronomy.[13] Ruth uncovered Boaz's bare feet when he was sleeping.[14] There are many other examples.

Shoes represent physicality. The foot gives the shoe life. The soul does the same for the body. It is the life force. And the body without life is dead. It is an inert blob. You don't relate to a corpse as a person. It isn't "Jimmy" anymore. It is "Jimmy's body." It looks like Jimmy. But it isn't. It isn't him. Jimmy is gone. The body is all that remains – so you bury it, farm it for organs, or donate it to science.

Shoes aren't perfect. They wear out. They hurt your feet. They give you blisters. They rub against your ankles. They break. And sometimes you do things in spite of them. (Did you ever try moving a couch in a broken flip-flop?) Shoes are limited.

Your body is limited, too. It is hungry, lazy, tired, and cranky. It doesn't like to get out of bed in the morning. It has to use the bathroom. It wants to have sex all the time. It gets distracted. It is hard to feel spiritual when your body is distracted.

And that is why the most intense spiritual experiences are barefoot.

Muslims take their shoes off to pray. Jews don't wear shoes on Yom Kippur.[15] The priests didn't wear shoes in Solomon's Temple. Many people take off their shoes when meditating. I am sure there are many examples. You have to step out of your body – or at least not get distracted – to be spiritual.

The relationship between spirituality and music works the same way. You can't have a spiritual experience with music if you are distracted. You have to listen. If you are angry, afraid, depressed, self-centered, arrogant, or self-absorbed you won't hear the music. And music can't affect you if you aren't listening.

### Boots

Boots are thick, hard, rugged, sturdy, and impenetrable. Nothing gets in. A good boot protects your foot from the outside world. That is good if you are shoveling snow, walking in the woods, fighting a war, or slam dancing in a mosh pit. It isn't good if you want to snuggle in bed with your beloved. Boots in bed are awkward, clumsy, weird, and get in the way of intimacy.

Is your body like a boot? It could be. It could block out the world and prevent you from connecting to other people. You can't be yourself when you are afraid, insecure, intimidated, or nervous. You can't express yourself. And you can't hear what other people are saying as well.

Many people are afraid of speaking in public. If you search for public speaking online, you will find many quotes that say that more people are afraid to speak in public than they are of death. Death is number two. I don't know if this is an urban legend or not – I couldn't find the study everyone cites – but many people I know are afraid of public speaking. And it isn't just a fear of speaking. Musicians, actors, salesmen, and politicians get stage fright, too.

You get sweaty hands, your mouth goes dry and pasty, you shake, and you have to go to the bathroom. Big neon lights flash in your head: "Oh my God, everyone is looking at me."

You cannot communicate when the "Oh my God" blinkers are flashing. You can say – "Man, I am really scared" – but that is about it. You can't be yourself. You can't listen either. Your brain shuts down.

You are self-absorbed when you are terrified. You stop thinking and listening. You think you are going to die – or at least you would rather die, it is easier – and you worry about what other people think about you. You know they think you are incompetent, ignorant, inadequate, or pathetic. And you can't openly exchange ideas when you feel that way.

You know what I am talking about if you ever had to talk, sing, dance, perform, audition for something, defend a paper, make a presentation, or look intelligent in front of a group of people. You cannot say what you want, the way you want to say it. You can't find the right words (or the right notes). You are too self-conscious, blocked, apprehensive, insecure, and you can't take your boots off.

It is like wearing boots on a hot day. You feel gross and your feet feel like prisoners. Your feet need to breathe. But for whatever reason you can't take them off. You suffer and think about your hot feet, but there is nothing you can do. You are trapped.

Fear, insecurity, terror, apprehensiveness, and nervousness are the spiritual equivalents of wearing your boots in bed. It doesn't work. You can't communicate. You can't express yourself. You can't listen. You aren't open. And when that is the case, music won't speak to you. You won't feel intimate with anything or anyone. You can't – your soul is stuck in a sock, behind a wall of leather, under a tongue, and bound by crisscross rows of waterproof laces.

### Six-inch Stiletto Heels

But boots aren't the only shoes. Imagine going to a European disco in mountain boots. It doesn't work. To dance you need shoes that speak sex. You need six-inch Stiletto heels, open-toed pumps, or platforms with fishbowls. You need a shoe that demonstrates your dominance and control.

Not everyone is afraid to speak, sing, lecture, or perform in front of people. Some people love it. If you do, you know the thrill, excitement, exhilaration, and fun of being self-confident and in control. You have the crowd in your hand. You can do no wrong. And big neon lights flash in your head, "Oh my God, everyone is looking at me."

Talk about a paradox. The world's biggest fear is your incredible high. No anxiety, cold sweat, clammy hands, dry mouth, or trembling – just power, control, and self-confidence. It is a rush knowing that all eyes are on you.

But you can go too far.

You can fall in love with yourself. Many people do. You – the unbelievable you – are the total, complete, and uninhibited center of attention. And that isn't any different than stage fright. You can't communicate or listen. You cannot be open to others. You are filled with yourself. You are still blocked. It is just a different pair of shoes.

Did you ever listen to a singer who was in love with the sound of his voice? It was embarrassing. Wasn't it? You cringed. You wanted to hide. You were embarrassed for him. He overdid it. It was obvious that he was showing off. And it was obvious that he was not in touch with anything but himself.

It was easy to tell, too. He lacked subtlety and sophistication or he stuck his subtlety and sophistication in your face. "Be quiet. Can't you see I am being expressive? You plebe."

This is the guy who ruins your hippie-love-in campfire experience. You know the type I mean. He doesn't shut up. He closes his eyes. He throws his head back. He is loud. He tramples over everyone else. And you know it is just a show. He isn't connected. You can't bond with him. He isn't open. He is too busy being a great singer and making the experience awesome. But it isn't. At least it isn't for anyone besides him.

### A Story About High Heels and Cages

I was in a great band when I was in college. We lived in Boston and most of the band was studying at the New England Conservatory. They moved to New York my senior year. I left the band to finish college, but we remained friends. I hung out with them after I moved to New York a year later. And my replacement was a cool guy, too.

They got big. They got signed to a major label. They had gigs at the major venues in New York. It was a big deal.

One big gig was at the Limelight in Manhattan. A gig at the Limelight was important. The Limelight was a church that was converted into a club. It was huge. It was massive. It was enormous. It had back rooms and hidden places in addition to a gigantic main stage and dance area. It was also sleazy and a haven for drugs – both users and dealers – and that was the reason it eventually shut down.[16] But in those days, the Limelight was the biggest thing going.

My friends told me to come. I was on the guest list. I had backstage access. I was cool.

I never went to places like the Limelight. It was not for me. I don't like dancing. I don't like dressing up. I don't like cologne. I don't get it. I don't like the music. I don't dig the vibe. The gig was a new experience. I hung out with my friends in the dressing room before the show. I felt like a celebrity.

It was time for them to go on. I went out front as they prepared and went on stage. The room was massive. A few thousand people were in the club and there was room for more, too. The show started. The band played.

They were great. I hung out in the back near the mixing console – that was cool enough for me – I didn't want to get lost in the pit. My plan was to go backstage after the show, hang with my friends, and go home.

The show ended and immediately – like the second it was over – the room went into disco mode. The band was just a warm up for dancing, the real event of the night. The music – bass pumping, four-on-the-floor, inane words, samples, and tons of keyboards – was blaring.

I stood there. I wanted to leave, but I couldn't. I watched. I never saw anything like it. It was hip. It was happening. It didn't get any better. (At least that was the hype.)

The club had black iron cages – large enough to hold a person – set up in opposite corners of the big room. A woman got into each cage. A bouncer locked her in. The cages were lifted about twenty or thirty feet up into the air by thick black metal chains that were suspended from the ceiling.

The women in the cages danced. They danced like mad. They were young and not wearing very much. I felt like an Iowa farm boy in the big city for the first time. I had never seen anything like it. It was very cool.

What do you think the dancers were thinking? Were they lost in the transcendence of the moment? Maybe. But they also had to be aware that they were the center of attention. How could they not be? Everyone was looking at them. I mean, how often do you see women hanging from the ceiling in cages?

They were objects. Everyone was looking at them. They knew it. And they loved it. You know they did. And that was the rush. It made dancing in a cage twenty or thirty feet in the air worth it. Dancing was better than the inane conversations they had when the dancing was over. Picture the scene:

"Wow. You are so cool. What was it like dancing up there?"

"Shut up. You are a moron."

"Did you see that? She spoke to me."

You get the point. If you are terrified – if you can't take your boots off – you can't listen. If you can't listen you can't communicate. And if you can't communicate you are not going to be moved or connected by music. It isn't going to happen. And it isn't going to happen if you are arrogant, self-centered, or egotistical either.

You can't wear mountain boots to a European disco. And you can't wear six-inch heels to a religious retreat.

### Barefoot

You need to take your shoes off to be spiritually intimate. You have to lose yourself.

Self-abandonment is the opposite of stage fright. It is the opposite of over-confidence. It is the opposite of limiting self-consciousness. It is liberating. You go for it. You get lost. And it doesn't matter – nothing does – except right now.

Think about the stupid faces a guitar player makes. He spent years worrying about his hair, his clothes, how to wear his guitar, how to pose, and how to stand. He made it. He looks cool. He is cool. And then he takes his solo. He gets lost. He makes lots of dumb faces. And he looks like an idiot.

For the guitar player, that feeling – "Oh my God, everyone is looking at me" – doesn't matter anymore. It is not important. His ego, fears, sex drive, and attitude are in the off position. He is in the zone. He is unlimited. He is barefoot. He can do anything.

And he communicates. A guitar player – post-performance – is a sweaty, smelly, dirty creature. He is gross. He is disgusting. But backstage everyone wants to be his friend. Everyone wants to talk to him. He communicated. He got through. He spoke to his audience. And the relationship isn't superficial. They want to be with him. They don't care if he smells. They are interested in him – his soul – they saw it and liked it.

Stewart Copeland – the drummer from the Police – writes about this. He sweats like a madman on stage. He likes to shower as soon as the show is over. It is a fetish and he can't function until he showers. He can't talk to anyone. But people want to talk to him. People love him. They connected and want to meet in person. So his bodyguards escort him straight from the stage to the shower. It is the only way. He can't walk to the shower alone. He won't make it. The show is still ringing in his ears. The audience hasn't even left the hall. And his posse takes him to the shower.[17]

That is the power of music and self-abandon. It doesn't matter if you are a musician, in the audience, listening to a recording, by yourself, or part of a group. You get lost. You go beyond yourself, your limitations, your ego, and your inhibitions. You abandon your body and get lost in the language of your soul. The externals don't matter. You are in the zone.

I didn't listen to punk, ska, reggae, or anything like that in high school. I liked heavy metal. But punk was big at that time and by college I was more sophisticated, ready to try something new, and old enough to get into clubs. My roommate loved Fishbone – the Bay Area ska band

– and took me to their show in Boston. Admission was only eight dollars.

The club was packed. The opening act was the rapper Schooly D (he was hysterical). Fishbone was next. They started their set and the place went nuts. The room was a sea of people bouncing up, down, and into each other. Slam, bang, boom – it was awesome. I went for it. Song after song I was slammed, pounded, and pummeled. I surfed the crowd. I banged into things. Everyone else did, too. It was intense. But it wasn't violent. No one was out for blood – even the ska-loving skinheads were peaceful.

It ended in a flash. Hours seemed like minutes. It was incredible. I was electrified. I was lost – at least for a few hours – and I was in the zone. Whatever it was, it was big. And it was tribal. We bonded. Everyone did. We were brothers. The concert was a primal musical experience. It was earthy.

And the experience isn't limited to concerts and clubs. You don't need a massive sound system or thousands of people to feel it. You can feel it anywhere and in any situation. You experience it around a campfire, in the car, or at religious services. That feeling – getting lost – is the first taste of spirituality in music.

The first time I realized that music and spirituality were connected was about twenty years ago. I was in Jerusalem. I had been there for about a month. The holiday of *Simchas Torah* was at the end of September that year. The streets were packed. There were mobs of people dancing and singing. The city was festive and alive. The bars were closed so there wasn't much else to do. I wandered around the Jewish Quarter with my new friends. They wanted to dance at one of the yeshivas. OK. Why not?

The yeshiva we went to was small. It was rundown, the walls were lined with books – many of them used, beat, and well loved – and the room was packed. We walked in. The music was deafening. I was immediately consumed by the dancing mob. I don't know how many people were crammed into that tiny space but it seemed like a lot. And they were all men; there were no women dancing in the yeshiva.

Two guys grabbed my hands a pulled me into a dancing circle. Around and around we went. The music was loud, the dancing was intense, it was hot in the room, I was sweating (everyone was), and the place stunk. My circle was just one of many going around at a breakneck speed. We were moving, running, sweating, and yet packed together and squashed. If you fell you were dead. A few guys carrying Torah scrolls were dancing in the center of the room. They had big sheets on their shoulders and over their heads. They were dancing with the Torah scrolls, spinning in circles, sweating, and the focus of all the action.

Someone from the crowd – I guess one of the leaders – grabbed me and pulled me into the center. He threw a *tallis* (the big sheet) over my head and handed me a Torah scroll. It weighed a ton. I stood there in the middle as the swirling mass of men went around and around. Ecstasy and joy, loud music, noise, and celebration: they were with me in the center of the circle. It was hard to dance because the torah was so heavy so I just sort of moved around, sweat, and took in the experience.

In the middle of all this – as I danced with the heavy Torah scroll – I realized something incredible. It was about the music and I was surprised I hadn't noticed it earlier. Maybe I hadn't noticed because the music was so loud. All of the music – and I mean *all* of it – was coming from men singing, stamping on the floor, and nothing else. There was no band, no instruments, no sound system, no DJ, no electronics, no acoustic guitars, no nothing. I was floored. This was my tribe. The experience was primal. It was tribal.

Think about it.

There were no women in the room – only men – and we danced and it was intense, loud, authentic, and unpretentious. It never occurred to me that Judaism could be this way. What happened to the boring services? Where was the inane, empty sermon? Was Judaism really this cool?

I felt like Alex Haley. In *Roots* (the story tracing his family's history) he goes to Gambia and finds his tribe. He was home. Israel was my Gambia. The Jewish people were my tribe. I was home too. We had our tribal customs, dress, and wild traditions. We danced with our books. We were able to go wild without a band, women, or any of the things considered essential when Western people celebrate. We were real, even if we wore conservative suits and black hats.[18]

The examples of self-abandon I cited above were accidents. They were freak events. The stars aligned, mystical forces converged, and something magical happened. But real spirituality is a skill. It is a muscle you learn to flex; you learn to access it and benefit from it. You lose yourself at will. You are in control.

And you do that by being self-aware. Self-awareness is discipline. It is something you practice the same way you practice a musical instrument. And self-awareness is the result of understanding two things about yourself: your nature and your character.

Nature. Your nature is you. It is what makes you tick. It is your personality and temperament. Are you social or territorial, pragmatic or spontaneous, emotional or analytical, grounded in reality or living in la-la land?[19] Self-knowledge is power. It lets you accept who you are. It explains how you feel in different situations. And it gives you the confidence to let go.

Character. Your character is how you react. It is how you respond to different people or situations. Do you get angry or can you stay calm? Are you petty or generous? Are you materialistic or happy with the things you have? Identify your strengths and work to improve them. Discover your weaknesses and find ways to fix them. Knowing your problems is power, too. You don't make excuses. And it gives you the confidence to let go as well.

Self-abandon is a goal. It takes effort and time. It is the result of practice and self-awareness. And it starts with being happy. Happiness is often an accident. But it doesn't have to be. True happiness is a responsibility.[20] It is something you practice and do. It is a button you press when you need it. And it isn't hard; it just takes practice and effort.

Happiness is the result of counting your blessings. When you appreciate the things you have, you feel happy. When you focus on the things you don't have, you feel unhappy.

Try it.

Make a list of things you have: friends, sight, coffee, legs – whatever it is. Think about those things. How do you feel?

Make a list of things you don't have: money, a loved one who passed away, steak. Focus on the pain of not having those things. How do you feel? Terrible?

You can't control how you feel. But you can control what you think about. Happiness is a skill. It takes discipline. Practice and learn how to do it.

Self-awareness and happiness are tools. They help you do a lot of things. Learn how to feel good and let go. Learn how to lose yourself in the music. Transcend. Go to amazing places.

But if that doesn't work, you can always take drugs.

# 4
# Music and Drugs

*I wanted to call this chapter Sex, Drugs, and Rock n Roll. But that was cheesy.*

I feel sorry for people who don't remember vinyl records. They don't know what they're missing. Buying digital music isn't cool. It is one-dimensional. It's missing that wow. Remember going to the record store and flipping through the big bins, finding the record you wanted, feeling the plastic, and wondering what was inside the packaging? It was so cool.

And records were awesome. They were big and colorful. It was a treat when the album cover opened up like a book (that extra flap was called a gatefold[21]). Record art was awesome, too, especially the groovy record sleeves, free posters, labels, colored vinyl, and other creative packaging. I loved opening a new record and fumbling through the extras.

But none of that exists today. It was a slow demise. Records took a while to die. The music industry tried to kill them with eight-tracks and cassettes. That didn't work. Tape was lame – it was clumsy and awkward. But digital succeeded. The industry shrunk the album until it disappeared. First came CDs and the packaging got smaller. Then it went online and music went virtual. MP3 downloads are cool – and convenient – but the magic is missing.

I remember when Tower Records near West Fourth Street in Manhattan converted from records to CDs. It was a sad day. I went there after work – I often did – and when I got there, the store was a mess. The remaining albums were out of their bins and in big piles on the floor. The workers were resizing the bins to fit CDs. I was depressed. It was the end of an era. But today? Forget about it.

The death of records also ended an essential right of passage. Everyone had a friend in high school – his name was usually Tom or Pete (in my case it was Tom) – and he was the first kid to grow his hair, use deodorant, and grow a moustache. His parents were cool and let him wear a leather jacket and ripped jeans. He listened to cool music. He wore boots. And he was the first kid to smoke pot.

Remember Tom? You went to his house after school. He had a little bag of stuff that looked like oregano. His parents were never home. You hung out in his bedroom. You listened to pretentious music (it was usually *Tales from Topographic Oceans* by Yes, *Rush: Exit Stage Left*, or Bob Marley. But Bob Marley was cliché). The albums were always double albums – the gatefold was key – and Tom emptied the bag onto the album, usually onto the inner part of the cover, near the fold. And an album cover was perfect because it had a smooth, glossy surface and a crease.

He separated the seeds. It didn't take long. And then he rolled up a joint, lit it, and passed it around. Remember that? That was high school in America.

# Music and Drugs

Tom also knew about music. He decided what music was cool and what wasn't. You trusted his judgment. And music was essential. You didn't hang out in his bedroom without it. When Tom was tired of Yes or Rush, he listened to Pink Floyd – usually *The Wall* – unless he was feeling crazy. If he felt crazy he listened to Pink Floyd's *Ummagumma* or *Hocus Pocus* by Focus. But music was key.

Why was music essential? Every high school stoner listens to music in his bedroom with his friends. Music and drugs go together.

But why do they go together?

High school stoners aren't the only people who think that music and drugs are connected. Think about the last rock concert you went to. The band played their set. The audience went nuts. The band played an encore. They played another one. The show ended. The main arena lights were turned on – that was your signal that the concert was really over (no more encores) – and you could see the cloud.

Remember the cloud?

The cloud was huge. It was thick. It left a haze in front of the stage. It covered the entire seating area. It was the symbol of a great concert. It probably still is. I remember thinking it was green – it wasn't, but it could have been.

And some bands, at least when they were on the road, spawned small industries. Jam bands like the Dead supported a mini economy of drugs, paraphernalia, bootlegs, love beads, and other merchandise. How are these things related?

And the connection isn't limited to rock n roll. Every jazz club, dance club, disco, and theater serves beer. They usually serve harder drinks, too. It is even true at classical music concerts – if you are chic you can get invited to the cocktail reception preceding the concert. The venues sell drinks and that is how they make most of their money. The musicians are happy that the venues sell drinks, too. They get to work.[22]

Why are music, drugs, and alcohol connected? (And let's be honest, alcohol is a drug.) The connection is universal and ancient. I don't think you can name an art form or period in history that didn't connect music, drugs, and alcohol – from the ancient Dionysus festival to the late-eighties rave scene in England – the connection is universal.[23]

Drugs are connected to spirituality, too. You wouldn't think that at first. But take a deeper look; you will see it is true.

The first I time I heard about drugs and spirituality was in books and interviews by William S. Burroughs. He wrote about Indian medicine men and how they used peyote, yagé, mescaline, and other drugs to predict the future, find lost objects, and have visions of God.[24] Burroughs was intriguing. His ideas sparked a lot of intense conversations about God, psychology, visions, altered-states, and drugs. But he was far out; he wasn't talking about mainstream religion.

Yet many religions – including small groups, sects, and cults but also large denominations, international groups, missions, mainstream beliefs, churches, temples, and organizations – involve alcohol and drugs as a part of worship. Drug and alcohol use are standard practice, oftentimes taken for granted, and usually considered safe and beneficial.

Catholics believe that Communion is a fundamental Christian practice and mandate that every Catholic receive it at least once a year (during the Easter season). Communion involves eating bread and drinking wine. Catholics believe that the bread and wine are transformed into the actual body, blood, soul, and divinity of Jesus.[25] Catholics don't get drunk from receiving Communion – it isn't about that – but it involves wine nonetheless. I think it is significant that a central act of faith for a believing Catholic involves alcohol. And Communion isn't limited to Catholics, many other Christian denominations practice Communion as well.

In India, many Hindus drink Bhang – made of milk, spices, cannabis, and other ingredients – and it is associated with the goddess Shiva. Some people smoke ganja in association with their worship of Shiva as well.[26]

Judaism uses wine as an important part of spiritual life. Friday night – the start of the Jewish Sabbath – starts with Kiddush (the spiritual declaration that the Sabbath is beginning). Kiddush is said over a cup of wine. A cup of wine won't get you drunk, but it will give you a buzz if you don't drink during the week. Wine makes you feel different. Feeling different is important to feeling the spiritual difference of the Sabbath.

An important part of Passover – the Jewish holiday celebrating freedom – is drinking four cups of wine. Four cups of wine is a lot to drink, especially if you don't drink all the time, and you feel it. You don't get drunk. But getting drunk isn't the goal. The goal is to feel freedom. And you do – after four cups of wine – it loosens you up.

Wine is drunk at other times in Jewish life as well including weddings, circumcisions, holidays, and many other occasions. And on Purim – in most communities at least – Jews are supposed to drink enough to blur the lines between good and evil.[27] [28]

I can list other examples, too. Hindu Shamans are said to use Datura; a plant that makes you see God.[29] Rastas, Middle Eastern Sufis, and others use drugs as part of their spiritual life as well.[30] But why? Why are alcohol, drugs, and spirituality connected?

Drugs and music are connected. Spirituality and drugs are connected. Music and spirituality are connected.

What is the connection?

To explain the connection, start with the following. Imagine a social gathering. It can be any social gathering: a family reunion, cocktail party, football game, concert, after-hours mixer at work, or anything. The one thing they almost all have in common is drinking.

Isn't that true?

What you drink depends on the type of people getting together. It changes depending on age, wealth, social status, or what you are trying to do. It isn't always drinking either, but some substance is almost always involved. Rich people in Manhattan drink expensive drinks in fancy glasses. Engineers drink elitist microbrewery beer. Fat white men drink cheap beer and throw the empty cans at the TV (how is that for a stereotype?). Misfit computer programmers drink mead. High school stoners smoke weed at Tom or Pete's house after school. Yuppies serve white wine at dinner parties.

And the phenomenon is universal. You drink in bars, dance clubs, parking lots, living rooms, campsites, outside, mid-afternoon, late at night, at parties, or at cheesy hotels in upstate New York. Substances are served, expected, or at least considered normal almost every time people get together.

Why?

A drink helps you relax. You loosen up. You can be yourself. A beer, glass of wine, mixed drink, or whatever helps. It calms your nerves. It blocks out your prejudices, misconceptions, and insecurities. It turns off some of your filters. And it helps you let go.

Relationships are initiated and deepened at social gatherings. That is usually the reason you get together. But if you are self-conscious and afraid to interact – or you cannot honestly interact – you can't connect. And relationships are built on connection. If you can't interact and connect, you can't build a relationship. It isn't going to happen. That is why lots of people will employ a mild social lubricant to help break the ice.

You can get carried away, and that isn't cool. You look like an idiot. You end up talking gibberish and wearing a lampshade on your head. It is funny if it happens once. It isn't funny if it happens all the time or if you fight or degrade other people. But I am not talking about those times.

Drinking and drugs are also tools to calm your nerves. You can't focus after a hard day at work. You can't focus if you are furious. Many people come home beat, take a beer from the fridge, and the beer puts life back into perspective. The traffic jam wasn't the end of the world. Office politics don't mean much out of the office. Thank God you have friends, family, and people who love you.

And that helps explain the connection between drugs and music. Music is powerful. It changes your mood. It makes you feel better.

But you have to listen to it.

It is hard to listen when you are angry, miserable, distracted, busy, or in a bad mood. A buzz before the concert, in Tom's bedroom, at the club, or wherever helps you focus. It lowers the static and lets you hear the music. Your problems, bad grades, stupid boss, mortgage, or love life don't seem as bad, complicated, confusing, overwhelming, or insurmountable. You can handle it. And you can listen. The music will do its job. You will enter the zone, experience its power, transcend, and forget the bad stuff.

And you can be yourself. Drinking and drugs help you let go. They negate your insecurities, fears, and ego. They help you relax. And they help you hear the music. You don't get in the way. Think of music as a social interaction – it is just you and the song. "Let the music be your master. Will you heed the master's call?"[31]

*In vino veritas.* That is Latin. It means, "In wine there is truth." It is attributed to Pliny the Elder. But some say the quote is much older and attribute it to the 6th century BCE Greek thinker Alcaeus. A similar idea exists in Chinese too – "After wine blurts truthful speech."[32] It is also found in the Talmud: "Wine goes in. The secrets come out." It is an old and universal idea. Alcohol is truth serum.[33] You get drunk. You can't stop talking. You speak your mind. And it can be embarrassing. Did you ever get drunk and tell a friend what you really thought? Oops.

Communication is built on honesty. You cannot communicate if you are hung-up, distracted, or uptight. You can't be yourself. And that is dishonest. You aren't yourself. But a little buzz gets you beyond your hang-ups. You let down your guard. You honestly communicate.

And think about communication when your language is music. Wow. It penetrates. It bypasses your intellect. It tackles your emotions. You hear it.

Take this idea further. Your closest relationships are with the people you are most honest, open, and comfortable with. No games. No pretentions. No nonsense. You are you: raw, as is, and unadulterated. You cry, laugh, yell, pick your nose, and you can be yourself. No fear. You don't hold back – you pass gas, criticize, tease, and speak your mind. You are honest, straight, open, and to the point. No holds barred. You act this way with family, parents, siblings, spouses, children, and best friends. You know each other. You understand each other. And you love each other.

Love isn't blind – that is a stupid cliché – it isn't true. Love is a magnifying glass for faults.[34] The most important people in your life know you the best. It isn't pretty. I once read a story about Richard Feynman, the Nobel Prize winning physicist. *Omni Magazine* called him "the Smartest Man in America." His mother said, "If that is the world's smartest man, God help us."[35]

Haha.

But the most important people in your life see past your faults as well. They love you. They know how beautiful you really are. They are aware of your potential. They rejoice when you are successful. (Don't worry; Mrs. Feynman was proud of her son, too.)

Spirituality is a relationship. It is built on the same principles as any other relationship.

Spiritual experiences happen when you are open and honest. No garbage. No games. You don't hold back. No fear. You are yourself. You cannot connect to God, energy, a force, or whatever you want to call it if you are insecure, dishonest, or intimidated. You can't be yourself and you won't feel connected. Even if you do, the experience is superficial and fleeting.

But the relationship exists if you want it. Do you want it? It is up to you. And even if you want it, can you be honest? Can you be yourself? Can you let your hair down? Are you ready to communicate?

And that explains the link between drugs, music, and spirituality. Drugs break down your walls. They loosen you up. They help you act natural. And they turn down the noise so you can hear the music. Music is a language – but it isn't just any language – it is a language that bypasses the intellect. It creates a direct and amazing connection. It creates intimacy. You hear the music – you are a part of the conversation – and you feel the relationship. That is what spirituality is.

This isn't a new idea. I gave you a lot of examples and I think most people sense it. It is an intuitive idea. The Bible mentions it, too. Look at this quote from the Book of Judges: "Wine gladdens God and man."[36]

Interesting. God *and* man – how so? It is easy to see how wine gladdens man. But what about God? God doesn't need a stiff drink.

Check out the Talmud. The Talmud explains biblical verses based on the Jewish tradition. And it explains that this verse is referring to the connection between drugs, music, and spirituality. How?

When man drinks, he *sings* praises to God.[37] What kind of praise? Not empty flattery. But the praise of a person after he drinks – i.e. the praise of a person who can let go. After a drink you are uninhibited. You are yourself. You are honest. And that is the ultimate praise you can give God. Being you. God made you. He loves you. He knows you. When you can be yourself – no BS – that brings God more joy than anything else you can do.

I don't want to be your mommy, preacher, or moral counselor – but it is important to note that I am not advocating drug use. I hope that is clear. My goal is to explain the connection between drugs, music, and spirituality. Be an adult. Don't try to read something into what I said. There is a huge difference between getting a buzz and going too far. It isn't cool to barf on your friends or pass out on the street. Don't be an idiot.

Combining music and drugs can be dangerous as well. Some music is violent or aggressively sexual. Music is an emotional language. It speaks to your soul. But it speaks to your inner animal, too. That can be a bad thing. You lose yourself and do things you regret or worse. Anger and sex are also emotions. Don't trigger those emotions with music. And don't use drugs as the excuse to let those energies in.

Drugs are tools. They are helpful. They help people listen. They help people find God. But you shouldn't need them and that is what I will talk about next. Music is powerful enough on its own – just make sure to listen.

# 5
# Music and Intuition

### The essence of feeling funky

Do you remember *The Jerk*? It was a great movie. Steve Martin played Navin Johnson, the white adopted son of black farmers. His family loved music. They felt it. They had rhythm. But Navin didn't. He didn't fit in.

Or so he thought.

One night – late at night – he discovered a new kind of music. He was alone in bed, eating a Twinkie, and listening to the radio. The station he was listening to played a song called *Crazy Rhythm* by the Roger Wolfe Kahn Orchestra. It was a very bland song. But his feet felt the pulse of the music. He didn't realize it at first, but one foot tapped gently into the other, it was an unconscious action.

And he felt it. He snapped his fingers. The rhythm took over his body. He went nuts. He got out of bed and danced around the house. He woke up his family. It was a transformative moment in his life. He left home and hitchhiked to St. Louis.

Rhythm is seductive. You feel a beat, groove, or pulse. You tap your foot or clap your hands. You bang your head. It happens all the time and it happens to most people. Most people don't hitchhike to St. Louis. But something happens. Music is something you feel.

And it doesn't matter what type of music you are listening to either. It happens when you listen to blistering funk, a waltz, a samba, rap, indie rock, fist pumping metal, a sonata, or whatever.

The music takes control. You lose control of your body. Your body moves with the music. Sometimes it is subtle. Sometimes it isn't. But you feel it. It happens to musicians. It happens to people who are not very musical. It probably happens to everyone. Not everyone feels the cool part of the beat. Not everyone follows complicated rhythms. But most people feel something.

Why does that happen? How does music take control? I am sure neuroscientists have a physiological description of the phenomenon (something happens via the ear-cerebellum-nucleus accumbens-limbic circuit[38]). But what happens on a deeper, spiritual level? How do you understand and relate to groove?

On a simple level, feeling a groove is similar to riding a bike. You flex the same mind muscles.

Do you remember when you learned how to ride a bike? Someone – probably your dad, mom, uncle, or sadistic older brother – told you what to do. He took you to a park, playground, cul-de-sac, or parking lot. He explained the idea. "Sit on the bike. Balance. Pedal. Try not to fall." He held the back part of the seat. You got on. He let go. And you fell over.

Why was that? You weren't stupid. The concept wasn't difficult. Why didn't you get it?

You didn't get it because you *didn't get it*. (Dig?) Understanding the concept isn't enough. You have to get it. Balance isn't something you explain. Balance is some-

Music and Intuition

thing you feel. And you either feel it or you don't. You can learn how to do it – and most people do – but at some point, the feel has to click. And until it clicks, all the explanations in the world won't make a difference.

Many things are like this. Juggling is like this. Did you ever try juggling? One of my kids learned how to juggle. He got good at it. He made it look easy. He had different types of balls, too; hard lacrosse balls, bean bags, bowling pins, fire sticks. I never learned how to do it, but my son left his balls lying around the house and I tried juggling from time to time. I wasn't very good at it.

One day he left his juggling balls on the kitchen table. I decided to see if I could figure it out. I started with two balls in one hand. I threw one ball. Threw the second. Missed the first and then missed the second. I picked up the balls. I thought about it and came up with a theory. The secret was rhythm – you have to time it so you are throwing the second ball when the first ball changes direction. Good idea. I tried again and dropped both balls. I tried again. I did it for about a half an hour. I kept dropping the balls. My back hurt from bending over so much.

But every once in a while I caught one. And sometimes I caught two in a row. And soon I was catching as many as I was dropping. I was getting good. After a while it started to click. I felt the rhythm. I can't explain what changed. I don't know what it was. But I got it. (I didn't continue the next day and I lost the knack. Juggling – like any skill – is something you have to practice.)

Understanding is not enough, at least not when it comes to a skill like riding a bike or juggling. It has to click. You have to get it. And getting it is a feel. You have to experience it. And even when you get it, you probably can't explain it. It is difficult to put a feel into words. Most words don't work.

Feeling a groove or beat is the same type of thing. You feel it, but you can't explain it. You can try. But your explanations usually fail.

If you want to try an experiment, ask a classical musician to play jazz. It is really funny.

The jazz feel is based on something called swing. Swing is based on the way you play eighth notes. Eighth notes are usually played straight; you subdivide the beat evenly. But in jazz you mess with the feel by delaying the second eighth note. The delayed second eighth note heightens your anticipation of the next downbeat. You usually emphasize the second eighth note as well, increasing the anticipation and sense of tension and release (i.e. swing).

You can explain it (I just did). You can notate it, too. But if you don't get it, you sound ridiculous. Classical musicians not schooled in jazz don't get it. They never experienced it. They don't feel it. And they sound like humpty dumpty when they play it. Dump, de-dump, de-dump. It is funny because it sounds very wrong.

But you can't explain why it sounds very wrong. It is difficult to articulate. He is doing everything right. He is playing the right notes. He is playing the correct rhythms.

But he isn't.

The feel is wrong. You can tell. He can tell. But he doesn't get it. It doesn't click.

That is the power of groove. It is intuitive. You can discuss it. You can try to explain it. But explanations and theory only get you so far. At some point, you either get it or you don't.

Music and Intuition

Intuition is deep.[39] It is the essence of getting it. It is the secret of bike riding, juggling, and feeling a groove. It is a deep connection to music. It is deeper than your emotions (see chapter 2). It transcends your intellect, too.

Intellect. Intellectual knowledge is information, ideas, and explanations. You analyze something and put it into words. It is something you articulate and it makes sense.

You use your intellect when listening to music. It is how you remember the name of a song, artist, genre, time period, and whether you like it or not. It is how you remember the words. It is the way you tell someone about it or how you teach someone to play it.

Some music is intellectual. It is academic, calculated, or testing a theory. It was written that way. The composer wanted you to think. And it is appreciated that way, too.

But your intellect is superficial. Possessing facts and information doesn't imply understanding. Did you ever study for a test, get all the answers correct, and still not know what you were talking about? Some people are book smart. I had friends who memorized the almanac, always won at Jeopardy, and filled out the Sunday crossword puzzle the way most people fill out a form.

But they weren't good at anything. Being good requires something more. That more is intuition.

And intuition is something you can't explain, at least not in an intelligent way. Intuition is about getting it. It is a feel or skill. It is a knack or expertise. And it is hard to describe a feel.

Think about it. The best musicians and athletes are rarely good teachers and coaches. They can't explain what they do. They feel it. They do it. But they can't tell you how. And they don't make sense when they try.

Groove is intuitive. You feel it. You don't feel it *per se* – a groove isn't emotional – but you do. The music speaks to you. You get it. You tap your foot, dance, or bang your head without thinking about it. It happens. It is like riding a bike or juggling. It clicks and you experience it. The groove takes over – it bypasses your intellect – and it is an experience. And that experience – if you go with it – is the gateway to self-abandon. It is the power of music. It is the reason you don't really need drugs to let go, you just need to listen. Music is powerful. And it can change your mood.

Your mood is in your head; it is the product of your thoughts. When you are upset, worried, distressed, annoyed, or on edge it is because you are thinking about your problems. You can't stop. One thing leads to another – the problem could be huge, overwhelming, massive, tragic, out of your control or small, manageable, or insignificant – but it is on your mind and dominates your thoughts.[40]

A good mood is based on the same idea, except that you count blessings instead of problems. And thinking about good things feels good.

You can control your thoughts. It is hard to do. It takes effort, will power, and it is a skill you have to learn. But you can do it. You can decide to think about the good things instead of the bad.

And sometimes it happens by accident. You get distracted. Think about the last time you were in a bad mood. You were ticked off. You were mad at the world. Someone switched your coffee with decaf. You got stuck in traffic. You were late for a meeting. You were venting, fuming, cursing, kicking things, and your face was red and flushed. And then you heard something funny. Maybe it was on TV. Maybe you overheard a conversation. Maybe someone made fun of how funny you look when you are angry. But whatever it was, it broke the ice. You laughed. You calmed down. You laughed some more. It took a while. And you felt better. The distraction shifted your focus and changed your mood.

My teacher, Rabbi Noah Weinberg, used to explain it like this: Imagine that you are sitting at a red light. You are driving your new car. Your new car is very expensive.

And then someone crashes into you from behind. You are furious. You want to kill him. But then he backs up and does it again. Twice? Rage. Fury. You get out of your car. You storm over to his. You knock on his window.

He rolls down his window. He is holding a gun. He points the gun at you. "May I help you?" He says.

Boing.

"No. No problem. Have a nice day. Sorry I was in your way." No more rage. No more fury. You walk back to your car. You are cowed.

What happened? Why the change?

The distraction (a lunatic with a gun) changed your perspective. You realized that your life was more valuable than your car. You thought about that and it changed how you felt.

Music is a distraction, too. But it is a sneaky distraction. It is intuitive. It speaks to your subconscious and bypasses your thought process. You feel it. You feel the groove. You move your body. You get lost in the music. And you stop thinking about your problems.

Music doesn't solve your problems. But it changes your perspective. It gets you focused on something else and changes your mood. It is able to do that because it doesn't compete with your thoughts. You are at the mercy of the music – not your thoughts – and the music takes you where it wants to go.

That change can be good. A good groove takes you to a good place. You think about the groove. You don't think about your problems. You feel good, let go, get lost in the music, and transcend. It can get you excited, too. That is the reason you hear music at football games, parades, and charging into battle. It gets your adrenaline flowing.

But it can be dangerous. Not all grooves are happy or pleasant. Some music is depressing. Some music can unleash your inner animal, and that isn't always good.

Musical taste is subjective and it is important to note that. I don't know if objectively evil or bad music exists. People say it does, but I don't know. I love the sound of a tritone.[41] The medieval church said it was the devil's interval. Does that make me a devil worshipper? I don't think so.

But it is fair to say that some music is violent or aggressive or sexual. It has the power to bypass your thought process like any other type of music. You can get lost in it as well. And it is wrong to use music as your excuse to act out sick fantasies. It is worse to use it as a license to riot, destroy things, or take advantage of other people. Music can do that. But it isn't about that.

Music is intuitive. It speaks to you on a deep level. You react to it without realizing it. It is powerful. It can overwhelm you. Use music to let go and get lost. Use it as a happy distraction. Use it to change your perspective. Use it to feel good. Use it to make other people feel good. Music can do that.

Turn off your mind, relax, and float downstream.[42] Clear your head, find yourself, transcend, and find God.

# 6
# Unity

*War, God, and your secret desire*

Most Stones fans remember the war between Mick and Keith. After more than twenty years of touring, controversy, drug busts, massive concerts, and great music the band unraveled. You heard about it in the press. Keith said something about Mick. Mick said something about Keith. Each side had his story. It was nasty.

Look at this quote from Keith about the beginning of the rift, when things first started to fall apart.

> It must have been pretty bad for anyone around us who worked on *Undercover*. A hostile, discordant atmosphere. We were barely talking or communicating, and if we were, we were bickering and sniping. Eventually, in the Pathé Marconi studios in Paris, trying to finish the album, Mick would come in from midday until five p.m. and I'd appear from midnight until five a.m.[43]

Sound familiar? Remember the Ozzy quote about the breakup of Black Sabbath? The Stones had the same problem: they stopped communicating. Mick and Keith said things in the press. They said things to other people.

They talked a lot. But they didn't say anything to each other. Zero communication. The problems grew and got worse, more serious, and more intense until the situation reached its breaking point in the mid-eighties.

But the Stones survived. Mick and Keith called a summit and broke the ice. They reached an understanding. The band went back on tour. But many bands don't. Many bands stop talking and never get back together.

A band is a team. The individual players form a unit. Each piece fits. And communication is the glue. Communication keeps the band together and working. Good communication distinguishes a good band from a great one. The band communicates on stage, in the studio, in rehearsal, or any time they make music.

And in a good band, the members can read each other's minds. The guitar player knows what the drummer is going to do. He can tell. The drummer knows what the bass player is thinking. Each member will adjust what he plays based on what he anticipates is going to happen. It is amazing to watch. Look at this quote from Miles Davis talking about his great group from the mid-1950s:

> But as great as [John Coltrane] was sounding, [drummer] Philly Joe [Jones] was the fire that was making a lot of stuff happen. See, he *knew* everything I was going to do, everything I was going to play; he anticipated me, felt what I was thinking.[44]

A good band communicates off stage, too. They live together, travel together, eat together, and do just about everything together. Sometimes they clash. Sometimes somebody says something stupid. It happens. But as long as they communicate, they stay together and solve the problems. The tensions, bad vibes, hard feelings, and backstabbing start when the band stops talking.

Communication is a powerful connecting agent – I mentioned that in chapter two – and it is true for both the speaker and listener. Communication brings people together.

But it is deeper than that. Communication creates a bond. It solves problems, removes barriers, overcomes obstacles, and creates common ground. And that common ground is unity. Unity – that harmonious, unified, feeling of oneness – is the basis of relationship. It is the basis of a band, team, business, partnership, family, or spiritual experience. Unity is that good feeling and the reason these things work. Nothing feels better than coming together, bonding, uniting, getting married, being part of something, or getting lost as a part of a greater whole.

But unity is fragile. It is easy to destroy. And that is because your natural reaction when you are angry, depressed, upset, or hurt is to stop talking. You bottle up your pain and frustration. You keep it in.

Think about the last time you were really mad. You didn't want to talk to anyone. No one could help you. You were mad at the world. And the less you talked, the madder you got. You let the pressure build, you didn't release the tension, and the problem got worse and worse. You thought in circles and found more reasons to be mad. You were ready to kill.

Depression is similar. Think about a time you were sad or down in the dumps. You wanted to be by yourself to brood. Alone. An island. You got lost in your head. Your problems got bigger and bigger and you couldn't think about anything else. The problems took over your life.

But when you spoke to someone, you felt better. Isn't that weird? You didn't need to solve the problem. You didn't need to confront your enemy. You just needed to get it out – even if getting it out was nothing more than malicious gossip – it helped. You felt better. Talking is a relief. It makes you feel better. It explains why the Stones talked to the press but not to each other. Talking to the press didn't solve their problems – they needed to call a summit to do that – but it helped. At least they could get the problems off their chests.

If you want to save the relationship, you have to discuss it in person. It isn't easy. It is a confrontation. You start off screaming. It can be nasty or intense. But at some point you talk. You don't have to solve the problem – you may really disagree – but talking gets you over the hump. You realize that your enemy is a human being too. You break the ice and move on.

And breaking the ice is the point. You want to be alone when you are upset. You don't want to feel connected to other people. So you stop talking. But talking – to anyone, even to a stranger – makes you feel better. It gets you out of your private world. And talking to the source of your problem is even better. It builds a bridge. It reestablishes the connection. And that connection is the road to unity.

People are social. People like being with other people. You need relationships – friends, lovers, family, colleagues, confidants, acquaintances. Some people like being alone. But even most loners have friends. You crave closeness and oneness. And the reason for that is spiritual. Your soul is longing for God.

Wow. That is heavy. What do I mean?

What is God? Up until now I have been calling God, "God, energy, a force, or whatever you want to call it." But that isn't fair. You need a definition. You can't discuss anything without defining your terms.

Years ago I was frustrated because I only knew a pop-culture definition of God: i.e. some sort of mythical-tooth-fairy-energy-thing. And based on that definition, I decided there was nothing, when you died you were dead, and that apathy was an art. But I was dishonest. Deep down I believed in God. When I was mad I yelled at God. When I was sad I complained to God. When I needed something I prayed to God. I believed in something. I just didn't call it God.

Different people have different ways of understanding God. Different cultures view God from different perspectives. You have to think about God and decide what it means to you. My definition is the Jewish definition. It is based on classical sources. It is in the Talmud, it is mystical, but it is practical as well. I thought about it for a long time and I think it makes sense.

God is not energy, a thing, Santa Claus, a bearded man in the sky, a sweet old man with a checklist, the goodness within you, or George Burns smoking a cigar in your shower. God doesn't sit on a cloud taking notes to see if you earned enough points to get into heaven. God is not a man. God doesn't have a gender.

God is the master of reality.[45] Everything that happens is a manifestation of what God wants. In simple language – God is the source of reality. Or more simply – God *is* reality.[46]

And your soul yeans for reality – your soul wants to live – and you feel it when you experience pleasure. Pleasure is a taste of God. And pleasure is all you want.

Does that sound weird or farfetched?

Try an experiment. Think about your goals. Think about the things you do. Why do you need friends? Why do you love your family? Why do you want to get married? Why do you want a career? Why do you want to make money? Why do you want to save the whales? Why do you want to get people to stop smoking, stop polluting, or stop fighting? Why do you want to make the world better? Why do you write music, books, poems, or post cute comments online? What motivates you? Why do you do what you do?

No matter what it is, your answer is probably something like: "It makes me happy. It feels good. It gives me pleasure." Sometimes it takes multiple steps, for example:

"Why did you post that offensive, obnoxious comment online?"

"I wanted to bother Boris."

"Why did you want to bother Boris?"

"Bothering Boris is funny. He gets angry. He makes stupid faces. It makes me laugh. And laughing gives me pleasure."

Do you get it?

You are wired to want pleasure. That good, warm, electric, ecstatic feeling is the only reason you do anything. It is the only reason you get out of bed, struggle, work hard, make sacrifices, or spend money. Pleasure feels great. It is real. And it makes you feel alive.

When you feel alive – when you are aware of how awesome life is, when you are aware of reality – you are aware of God. If you don't like the word God, don't call it that, but that is what it is.

Sometimes you get confused. Sometimes you fall for illusions. Illusions – things like over-indulgence, infatuation, status, power, cults, and drugs – feel pleasurable at the time. But the pleasure doesn't last. In the end you feel cheap, empty, degraded, selfish, and ripped off. But real pleasure – simple pleasures like eating or smelling a flower or more sophisticated pleasures like love, meaning, doing the right thing, leadership, creativity, and transcendence – feel great.

The more sophisticated pleasures like love, leadership, and doing the right thing involve other people. Isn't that interesting? Pleasure is about unity. It is about connecting to something or someone else. It is about getting beyond self. It is about being at one with reality. And it feels good when you make the connection.

Transcendence is a relationship, too. It is a spiritual relationship. You don't have to meditate to experience transcendence, but many people do. And when you talk to people who meditate, they invariably talk about nothingness. Nothingness is a goal of meditation.[47] Isn't that odd? Meditation is hard work. Why spend years learning a skill in order to experience nothing?

Nothingness isn't the goal. Nothingness is a tool. You experience nothing to make way for something. You are in the way. You need to get out of the way. Nothingness does that. When you are in the way, you aren't experiencing God, you are experiencing a lot of you. And that isn't transcendent. It's self-indulgent. It isn't a relationship. It is spiritual masturbation.

And music – remember music, we were talking about music – is a tool for effective meditation.

Music is language. Like any language, it is a way to communicate. And like any language, it brings people together, builds relationships, and creates a feeling of oneness or unity. But unlike any language, it has a special advantage. It bypasses the intellect, speaks to the emotions, and works on an intuitive, subconscious level. And that advantage makes it the perfect tool to create a relationship with something deep and unknowable like God.

In the Bible, the prophets used meditation as a tool to find God. Music was an important part of the experience. That makes sense. Music is an important part of meditation.

> A repetitive melody is very much like a mantra, and it can be used to banish extraneous thoughts and clear the mind for the enlightened state. An important category of classical meditation is the path of the emotions, rather than through the intellect or senses. Since music can work very strongly on the emotions, it is particularly useful for this meditative method. Other sources state that music is the language of the spiritual world, and that through music, one actually communicates with the soul.[48]

Music works. It works because it is a unique language. It works because you are wired for unity. You want to connect to other people. You want to connect to God. And music does those things.

The proof is in the pudding. Music makes you feel connected. You feel connected to the musicians. You feel connected to the other listeners. You feel connected at a campfire. You feel connected at a concert. You feel connected when you are dancing. You feel connected when you are singing. You feel connected at religious services. You feel connected when you are stamping your feet at a football game.

Connecting feels great. It is what you want. It is the way you are made. It is at the root of most pleasures. It is the basis of spirituality. And it is the reason why music and spirituality are so closely related – they have the same goals: oneness, closeness, and unity.

# 7
# Sex

*Forget the drugs and rock n roll – music, spirituality, and sex are related.*

Musicians are irresponsible, unkempt, dirty, creatures of the night. Some take drugs. Some are incubators for disease. Most don't look good. Many are unhealthy, hairy, tattooed, sweaty, and disgusting.

Yet they are the most sexually active people on the planet.

How can that be? What sane, rational, normal, decent person would sleep with a musician?

And the sexual exploits of musicians are famous. Stories and legends abound. Groupies have written books about their experiences. Bands have immortalized their favorite adventures in song. People have made movies about musicians and sex.

It gets better, too. Musicians and hyper-sexuality may be rooted in science; some scientists assert that musical ability has an evolutionary basis.

Think about that.

It makes sense to link music and evolution. Musicians and their overactive libidos make for the most prolific breeders, and successful breeding is the lynchpin of evolutionary theory. If you breed, you survive. And your genetic mutations survive as well.

> [The cognitive psychologist Geoffrey Miller writes that] Jimi Hendrix had "sexual liaisons with hundreds of groupies, maintained parallel long-term relationships with at least two women, and fathered at least three children in the United States, Germany, and Sweden. Under ancestral conditions before birth control, he would have fathered many more." Robert Plant, the lead singer of Led Zeppelin, recalls his experience with their big concert tours in the seventies: "I was on my way to love. Always. Whatever road I took, the car was heading for one of the greatest sexual encounters I've ever had." The number of sexual partners for rock stars can be hundreds of times what a normal male has, and for the top rock stars, physical appearance doesn't seem to be an issue.[49]

Women went nuts for the Beatles – watch the footage from the old TV shows or look at the photographs – screaming, crying, hysteria, fainting, you name it. Sociologists and psychologists have reasons to explain the phenomenon. People have written books about it. But whatever the sociological, psychological, or other scientific reasons, it was music that made the girls go crazy. They went nuts for a band. They didn't go nuts for an author, engineer, scientist, painter, talk show host, movie star, or anyone else.

And music and sexuality is not new. The connection isn't limited to rock n roll. The classical masters created a sexual frenzy in their day. A great example is Lisztomania. The term was coined in the 1840s to describe the hysterical reaction women had to the music and performances of Franz Liszt (some say it was the inspiration for the term "Beatlemania").

> [Liszt was] a strutting, manipulative, priapic rock star for the Romantics, with a sexual magnetism that set off what the poet Heinrich Heine dubbed Lisztomania, a condition in which swooning female fans collected his cigar butts to secrete in their cleavages.[50]

Liszt was a classical pianist. (So much for those who claim that rock n roll – as opposed to classical music – is the music of the devil. The devil was hard at work in the classical era, too.)

Sexuality was big in the jazz era as well. (The word "jazz" was probably first used as a slang term for sex. So were terms like boogie-woogie, gig, and swing.[51]) The great bassist/composer Charles Mingus enumerates his sexual exploits at length and in graphic detail in his autobiography, *Beneath the Underdog*. Miles Davis writes about sex in his autobiography, too. You can find many examples.

And middle-aged women still go crazy for Tom Jones and Barry Manilow. Figure that out.

Most musicians have stories and the phenomenon isn't limited to celebrities. Even no-names and guys in bar bands have war stories. And music and sex isn't just about male performers and their adoring female fans. Many women have made long and successful careers playing off sexual energy and roles, using sexual themes and pushing borders, boundaries, and limits.

Some music – irrespective of the performer – is sexual as well. Consider funk, techno, trance, rave music, or the pulsating, syncopated, percussive intensity in tribal grooves. The music oozes sex. And the best musicians/composers manipulate rhythm – whether they realize it or not – and stimulate sexual tension, release, yearning, and longing.

Sexuality in music is obvious and powerful. It is so powerful, that some religious groups even prohibit men from listening to women singing. The singing female voice is seen as too erotic, too stimulating.

Music and sex are related. That much is obvious. But is that relationship spiritual?

I think it is. Music and sex are connected, the connection is spiritual, and it is rooted in your longing for closeness, oneness, unity, and intimacy. In the last chapter I mentioned that your soul is longing for God. You are wired to connect. You want reality. And the greatest pleasures – like love, doing the right thing, creativity, and leadership – involve other people.

Take that idea a step further – group experiences trump private experiences every time. Group experiences are king. A live concert is better than a recording. Most people agree. And that is why a concert costs more than an album (with some bands, a concert ticket costs more than their entire collection). Sports, too. You pay a lot of money to see a game live, at the stadium, and in person. There is nothing like screaming in unison with fifty thousand of your closest friends. You bond. You feel a rush. You don't want to leave. It is cathartic. And it is communal.

Spirituality is similar. The most intense spiritual experiences are communal. Nothing beats a gospel choir. The energy and mood is palpable. You feel it. You touch it. It is amazing. Or imagine how lame the hippie-campfire-love-in-experience would be if you were alone. It could be a positive meditative experience – maybe – but it is nothing like connecting with other people. There is something wonderful about coming together. And Yom Kippur and Simchas Torah are the highlight of the year for many Jewish people. They are community events. Connecting with other people is what makes these experiences special. Eating a sandwich feels great. So does smelling a flower. But they do not compare to bonding with other people. Connecting with other people is a rush: and the closer or more personal the connection, the greater the rush. And the most intense expression of that rush is marriage.

Most people do not want to be alone. They crave companionship, closeness, intimacy, and relationships. They date. They go to bars. They try to meet other people. They join online dating services. And most people start as soon as they hit puberty. Dating is a sign of maturity. It makes you a grownup.

Your first attempts are awkward and embarrassing. You fumble. You say stupid things. You fall for the wrong things. But most people eventually figure it out. You pop the question and get married.

And marriage is intense. It is a commitment. It involves your entire extended family. It is expensive. It is a big deal. And the concept of a marriage – what a good marriage should be – is stronger than any other relationship in your life, including the relationship with your children. You choose your spouse. You don't choose your kids. You commit to spending the rest of your life with the person you marry. You are stuck with your kids. That is how it works.

But in spite of the commitment – and the fear of commitment – most people get married. At least they try

– they know they should. Even rock stars – those free spirited, effective breeders – attempt it. Some may not officially call it a marriage *per se*. But it is.

And they get married because marriage is an intense expression of unity. Unity is what you crave.

Marriage is not a partnership. Partnerships don't work. Partners are never happy. You invest fifty percent. You expect your partner to invest fifty percent, too. But he doesn't. You work hard. Your partner doesn't work hard – not as hard as you do – and you resent him. He is a bum. If you think your spouse is your partner, and you expect fifty percent, you are going to be disappointed.

Marriage is not a legal agreement or sexual contract either. It has a legal component. The legal component is significant. But if you think of your marriage as a contractual agreement you will be dissatisfied. Marriage isn't about that.

Marriage is a union. The Jewish mystics describe it as two souls uniting, creating a new unit. Two people become one. Your marriage is successful when you know you are united. You are the same. You don't wait for your spouse to live up to his or her fifty percent. You give. You expect nothing. And you get back more than you can imagine.

Put the pieces together: your soul is longing for unity, marriage is an expression of unity, and that explains why your sex drive is so powerful. The sex drive is the physical manifestation of your spiritual longing for closeness and oneness.

Wow.

The sex drive is physical, but it has a spiritual root. You are longing to connect. Your soul is longing to unite. You want unity. And your sex drive is an actualization of your spiritual longing and desire to unite and become one. It's just in a physical form.

Sex is at its best when you are married, when you are committed, and when you are with someone you love. You committed to become one. Your marriage is an *expression* of unity. Sex within marriage is an *experience* of unity. You experience the idea you expressed getting married. It is the realization of your spiritual longing and desire.

And that is why your sex drive is so powerful. It is at the root of how you are made. You are longing to become one. You are longing for reality. You are longing for God. Your sex drive is a manifestation of that.

Sex is not just a physical sensation. It isn't like eating. You can eat alone. You can't have sex alone. You wouldn't be ashamed if someone walked in while you were eating lunch. You would be ashamed if someone walked in while you were having an intense personal experience. Shame. Embarrassment. Why? Who cares? You are experiencing a pleasurable physical feeling. It is just like eating a cupcake.

Except it isn't.

Eating a cupcake isn't an expression of unity. Sex is. You know it is. And that is why it is humiliating to do it alone. You are supposed to connect to another person. Not yourself. The physical sensation is pleasurable. But the situation isn't. It is missing the spiritual component. And you feel shame when you get busted.

Do you get it? You are longing for God. You want to become one. You are dying for unity. Your soul is screaming and craving oneness. Your body feels that, too. And the most obvious oneness is sex – especially in marriage – when you physically connect with another person.

Sex is spiritual. You can misuse, abuse, and misunderstand it. But if you keep it within the context of a committed, giving, and loving relationship – a relationship that is an expression and manifestation of unity – you experience oneness on every level. Sex can be transcendent and an experience of God.

But this isn't a book about sex.

I mentioned that communal experiences are amazing. They are amazing because you feel alive. You know that the experience is bigger than the number of people involved. Gestalt. One plus one equals three. Big. The result is greater than the sum of its parts. It is *it*. You are beyond self. You are unlimited. You are in the zone. And that zone is difficult to find on your own. Yes, most people have had amazing private moments. They exist. But they are not the same. The private moments do not compare to the intensity and intimacy of community. And that intimacy – that awareness of something beyond – is an awareness of God.

As you probably understand by now, music brings you to an awareness of God as well. Music is spiritual. It bypasses the intellect. It speaks to the heart. It is something you intuit – it isn't cognitive – it is something you get. These factors give it the ability to break down barriers, remove blocks, and bring people together.

And that explains how music and sex are connected. Sex is the physical manifestation of your spiritual longing for unity. Music is the language of unity. Music and sex tickle the same pleasure centers. They do the same thing. They bring people together. And people want to be together. They are longing for God.

The musician is the epicenter of incredible energy. He wields a lot of power. He speaks the language of unity.

Spiritual and sexual forces converge around him. You don't care if he smells, sweats, or doesn't wash his clothes. Your conversation is so much deeper than the bland, superficial niceties of pleasant society. Musicians are aware of this energy. They harness it and sleep with adoring fans. Madonna put on leather and sold a lot of records.

But in the hands of a master musician – or in the midst of a communal experience – the music is a bundle of spiritual, sexual, and intuitive energies. It bypasses your emotions. And it gives you an experience of God.

# 8
# Everybody Prays
### Music, prayer, and the lack of atheists in foxholes

I mentioned in chapter one that music is a universal aspect of spirituality. Almost every religion, group, sect, tribe, cult, or mystical gathering involves music as part of its worship. It doesn't matter if the service is formal or informal. It doesn't matter where the service is held. Music is central to the experience. The style of music could be serious, fun, meditative, interactive, spontaneous, improvised, or structured. It doesn't matter. But there has to be music.

And in particular, music is an essential aspect of prayer. Prayer is part of an active, regular, and daily spiritual relationship – at least it should be – it helps you transcend your limitations and forge a relationship. Music helps you pray better. It creates intimacy and makes you feel connected. And it is inspirational.

Everybody prays. Some people like the structured rigor of an organized system. Others prefer a more organic, intimate connection. Some only pray in times of crisis. But regardless, prayer is something most people do.

And there is no such thing as an atheist in a foxhole.

Imagine a foxhole (or reread *All Quiet on the Western Front*). You sit in a trench. Your trench is about three or four feet deep. Someone – the enemy – sits in a trench nearby and wants to kill you. He shoots, lobs grenades, and fires cannons at your trench. He hits someone from time to time. It rains. After a few days, your trench is filled with about a foot of water mixed with blood, guts, disease, and whatever else. You cannot leave until there is a lull in the fighting or another group comes to relieve you.

But it gets worse. One tactic of trench warfare is called "softening up" the other side. Before an army launches an offensive, they bombard the enemy with an assault of artillery, bombs, shrapnel, and gunfire. Their objective is twofold: to take out important strategic positions and to terrorize the other side.

Pretend that you are sitting in a trench. You are cold, tired, hungry, nervous, and the other side starts softening you up. Bombs land nearby. The ground shakes. You feel intense heat. You hear people in pain, screaming, moaning, and slowly dying. It goes on for hours and hours. You want it to end except that you don't want it to end – when it ends the other side will launch their offensive and you will have to fight or die.

Yikes.

Do you think you would be scared? Do you think you would pray?

Of course you would pray. You can't do anything else. You can't leave. You can't move. You can only turn to God. And you pray to God with everything you have. "Get me out of here. Now."

In a situation like that you don't think. You don't rationalize. You don't remember your philosophy lecture from college. You don't wonder about the existence of God or the effectiveness of prayer. You pray. And you beg God to save you.

In 1982, President Reagan proposed a constitutional amendment to permit organized prayer in public schools.[52] The effort failed. But during the debate, someone noted the following; "I don't understand the debate. As long as there are math tests there will always be school prayer." And he was right. For a kid, a math test is like sitting in a foxhole. He is terrified. He could fail. It is too late to study. So he prays. It is a natural thing to do.

People turn to God in times of crisis. Do you remember the headlines just after 9/11? They talked about God, prayer, hope, and faith. America got very religious – for about a week – people talked about God, the current and former presidents prayed together in church.[53] It was a heavy time.

In times of trouble, crisis, fear, or desperation you naturally turn to prayer. You don't make a pragmatic decision. You don't think, "Well, just in case – you know on the off chance – that God really exists, I might as well pray. Just in case." You don't think like that in the heat of the moment. You don't wax philosophical.[54] You are too busy, distracted, devastated, upset, or out of your head to meditate on the possible existence of God. You cry out in prayer.

You pray when you are terrified – you don't think about it – you do it. And that is because you believe in God. It is a belief that is ingrained in your psyche. It is deep. It is in you. You believe God will hear you and help. And that belief is so strong; prayer is a natural instinct in times of crisis. It doesn't prove that God exists. But it proves something about you. Think about it. It is an interesting thing to figure out.

If you don't think you believe in God – and maybe you really don't – try the following test and see for yourself.

Prayer is silly if God doesn't exist. It is just words. You are talking to yourself. Praying may have a psychological benefit, but it doesn't mean anything, do anything, or magically affect another person. It is just thoughts.

And if that is what you believe, try this experiment:[55] pick a person – someone you really love, someone important in your life – and pray that he dies a horrible, terrible death. Pray that he burns to death in a fire, gets hit by a car, gets a terrible disease, or gets struck by lightning. Be creative.

Can you do it?

If you can't do it, why not? It is just words. He will never find out. I won't tell him. Are you superstitious?

Some people say, "I can't do it because I don't like to create bad energy." Really? Be honest. Bad energy is just another way to say "God" without sounding religious.

Some people say they don't like to think bad thoughts about other people. But again, be real. When you are mad – like really mad – you don't have a problem thinking bad thoughts. You think terrible things. "That dirty rat. ARRGHH. I hope he dies. NOW."

Think about it and decide for yourself. If you can't do it, why can't you do it? What does that say about what you believe? I think it proves that you believe in God. Again, it doesn't prove that God exists. But it proves something about you. You believe it. You feel it. And that is something to think about.

But there is more. You don't just believe that God exists. You believe that God can deliver. You believe that God will answer your prayers.

Everybody Prays

And God always answers prayers – one hundred percent of the time – no prayer ever goes unanswered.

In 1994, Hamas terrorists kidnapped Nachshon Wachsman – an Israeli soldier – as he was hitchhiking home from a base in Northern Israel. Hitchhiking is normal in Israel and the terrorists wore yarmulkes, placed a Jewish bible on their dashboard, and listened to Hasidic music in order to trick someone into trusting them. It worked.

Nachshon was kidnapped on a Sunday. The terrorists said he would be killed that Friday evening if their specific list of demands weren't met. The Israeli government made a commitment to find him and free him. And the Israeli public prayed.

The Chief Rabbi of Israel instructed everyone – including school children – to say three chapters from the Book of Psalms every day. Nachshon's parents received about 30,000 letters from people saying they prayed for their son. And about 100,000 people gathered at the Western Wall – Judaism's holiest site – on the day of the deadline to pray for Nachshon's release.[56]

No one in Israel knew it at the time, but Israeli intelligence knew exactly where the hostage was being held. They knew who had him, where the building was, and the room he was in.

Israeli Prime Minister Yitzchak Rabin ordered a rescue attempt for Friday night. But the rescue failed. Nachshon was killed along with the mission's commander. Three of the terrorists were killed as well.

What happened? How did the rescue fail? Didn't thousands of people pray for his release?

God always answers prayers – no prayer ever goes unanswered – but sometimes the answer is "no." Nachshon's parents understood that as well. At the funeral, his father asked the rabbi to mention the "no" during his eulogy.

It isn't that God can't deliver. God can deliver. But for some reason he doesn't want to. If your father was a multi-millionaire and you asked him for ten dollars to see a movie, you would expect him to give it to you. He has the money. He can afford it. And you would be shocked if he said no. "Why did he say no? He loves me. He's rich. Why not?" Obviously, he has a reason. And if you were really shocked, you would do everything in your power to figure that reason out. Why not dad? What are you trying to tell me?

Maybe you prayed for something that isn't good for you.

When you were a kid, why didn't your parents give you unlimited access to candy? Children love candy. Candy makes kids happy. And your parents want you to be happy. Were your parents the exception? Were they evil, mean, sadistic, or horrible people?

Unlikely.

Your parents set limits because they loved you: you had to first finish your vegetables, you could only have one piece at a time, you couldn't have soda too. You cried. You begged. But your parents knew better – and as an adult you know they were right – but as a kid you were miserable.

Not everything you want is good for you. When I was in high school, I saw a news report about a guy who won the lottery. He won a ton of money. At the time, his wife wanted a divorce. He had a girlfriend, too, and she wanted to leave him. But then he won millions. His wife wanted him back. His girlfriend decided she wanted to stay. Life was great.

He decided to marry his girlfriend. I saw the wedding on TV. They spent a fortune on the reception. She wore a veil with diamonds in it. It was a beautiful wedding.

But do you think he is still rich today? I doubt it. Many lottery winners go broke. It is a common problem. Winning all that money isn't good for them.[57]

You can ask God for millions of dollars, a big house, fame, a new car, or a date with Mary Jane. And God can deliver. He has the money, connections, clout, and ability to make things work out the way you want them to. But that doesn't mean He will do it. The money, house, fame, car, or date could be a disaster for you. It could ruin your life.

Your job – when God says no – is to ask yourself why. "God can deliver. He wants me to be successful. He wants me to be happy. Why did He say no?" Maybe the thing you want will ruin your life. Maybe you can't handle it. Maybe you need to learn a lesson. Maybe you need to face a challenge and overcoming that challenge will make you a better person. It could be anything.

Prayer isn't a game. You can pray for anything, but you have to be real. You have to be clear and certain about what you want. You have to know why you want it. God's "no" may be because you are insincere, flippant, disingenuous, unfocused, or confused. Maybe your thoughts are vague or ambiguous. Maybe you don't know why you really want it. Maybe you are unsure what to do with it. And if that is true, God's "yes" won't help you. You will squander your big opportunity.

Prayer is part of an active relationship with God. Look at the answers you get – whether yes or no – and try to make sense of them. What is God telling me? Is this a test, a challenge, an opportunity, a message? Do I get it? Am I real? What should I do differently?

A relationship is real. It isn't one-sided. And it isn't something you only go to when you are desperate. You invest in a relationship. You get out of it what you put into it. A relationship is work and it isn't easy. And in your relationship with God – like in any relationship – you won't always like the answers you get.

But you should.

The answers are in your best interest – they are good for you – and that is what you really want: even if you are not mature enough or capable of understanding that at the time. You hated your parents when they didn't give you candy, let you smoke, let you drive by yourself, or have unlimited freedom. But now you know better.

A good relationship is built on effort and communication. A relationship with God is the same. Prayer is how you communicate. If you want a good relationship, you have to communicate regularly. You won't always feel like it. You won't always want to. You won't always be inspired. But it is like learning a musical instrument: inspiration doesn't make you great, regular practice makes you great. The best musicians don't wait for inspiration. If they did, they would never be inspired. You don't have to pray – you can wait for a crisis – but if you wait, you will rarely be inspired. You will miss out on an amazing spiritual relationship. And that is a waste of the power of prayer.

Music is an essential aspect of prayer. It is the language of the soul. It speaks on a deep, intuitive level. It connects to your emotions and you are often unaware of what it is doing to you. It changes your mood and inspires. It initiates a relationship between the musician and listener.

And as a regular part of prayer, it does all these things as well – except that now you are talking to God.

Music makes prayer real. It brings God into your life. It makes God a part of your consciousness and awareness. And it is a way to make prayer regular and consistent. You won't always be inspired. But with music you are more likely to transcend your limitations, forge a relationship, and feel connected. Look back at the end of chapter two: Music – as a language – skips the dry intellectual exchange of information, "What is your name?" "Where are you from?" And gets straight to the point. It relaxes you enough to hug a total stranger. It speaks in a way that isn't intellectual. You probably don't know all the words to your favorite song – and it doesn't matter – the words are secondary. The important thing is the connection. The music speaks to you.

Try it out. You pray in times of crisis. You are clear – there are no atheists in a foxhole – and you feel it in your gut. Terror is not a good feeling, but clarity is. Music gives you clarity. It reveals things you believe but don't usually see. And if you listen, you bypass fear and go straight to your gut.

Most religions understand that already. Music - regardless of style, structure, intensity, or mood – is central to the spiritual experience. Most people know that too. Music is the language of the soul. It takes time and effort. You won't always want to do it. But the relationship is worth it.

# 9
# The Bull, the Horns, and Something to Grab

Missed opportunities, joy, and the spiritual dimension of growth

I once knew a great drummer. He was awesome, influential, and well connected. His resume was a who's-who list of the biggest names in rock and jazz. He liked me. And better, he liked my guitar playing. He wanted me to audition for his band. Wow. His band was a big deal. The gigs were big and the best players in town were in his band. I was thrilled; it was a very cool opportunity.

I went to the audition – it was for the new guys he was trying out. I was the only guitar player. He was auditioning a few guys on horns and an awesome bass player, too. The bass player couldn't read music – but that didn't matter – it just meant that someone had to show him the parts. Not a big deal.

I was excited to try out but I didn't bother learning the material. I was given the charts a few weeks before the session. I had more than enough time to look them over. But I couldn't be bothered. I played well, the drummer liked me, and I thought I could wing it.

Bad idea.

At the audition the drummer asked me to show the bass player the parts. Oops. I was first figuring the parts out myself.

The drummer was upset. "You didn't learn my music?" He said. And that was it. It was over. I was out. No gig. No connections. No bonding with the killer bass player.

I was such an idiot. The music was not difficult. It was easy to learn. But I couldn't be bothered and now it was over.

And that is called a "missed opportunity."

Missed opportunities stink. You blew it, you know it, and you missed out big. Maybe you were afraid to take a risk. Maybe you thought something better would come along. Maybe you were lazy or distracted. Maybe you didn't prepare. Whatever the reason, you missed out, felt like a loser, and wanted to kick yourself.

You probably still do.

Music is an opportunity. It has a lot to offer. It has many advantages – I described many of them already: it is a special language, it bypasses your intellect and speaks to your emotions, you connect to it on an intuitive level, and it is related to prayer, meditation, and sex. If you listen, music will bring you to a special place. It is an opportunity for joy, spirituality, and growth.

And spirituality – like I mentioned in chapter two – is a relationship. You use the same words to describe it: love, connection, intimacy, unity, and oneness. You long for it and feel empty without it. Relationships and spirituality tickle the same pleasure sensors. They are different in that a relationship is a connection with another person. Spirituality is intimacy with God; you connect to reality, feel it, and know it. But otherwise they are similar.

Music, relationships, and spiritual experiences are great. But they are not goals. Music, relationships, spiritual experiences – and many other experiences and pleasures as well – are tools. They help you achieve your purpose in life. They make you feel good.

In chapter six I mentioned that pleasure is a taste of God. Pleasure is your goal. Your soul yearns for pleasure. It is the reason you need friends, family, and love. It is why you chose your career, go to work, and try to make money. It is why you want to save the whales, care about the environment, fight for justice, and try to make the world better. It is why you eat baloney. It is your root motivation. You do the things you do because you want to be happy. You are wired for pleasure.

Music, relationships, and spiritual experiences are vehicles for pleasure. They make you feel good. And that is why you want them, chase after them, and spend so much money on them. You want to be happy. These tools work. They can make you happy.

But you have to be aware. You have to do something. And that is the opportunity you don't want to miss. It is the secret of music. It is how to make music spiritual. And it is the secret of spirituality as well.

Whenever you listen to music – and you feel great, enter the zone, get lost in the music, and connect on an intuitive level – at that moment you have to stop.

Stop and say to yourself, "It is great to be alive."

Do it. Do it at that point. Do it when you feel it. Make the moment real.

Try it. It is not a buzz kill. It is not antithetical to the animal primacy of the moment. You are not over-intellectualizing the experience. You probably think it anyway. But now – even if it is just for flash – seize the moment. Internalize it. Make it real. And take it with you. The opportunity will end with the song – it is fleeting – but don't miss the point. Reflect, meditate, and reconnect with your purpose. You achieved your goal. It was pleasurable, and pleasure is a taste of God.

Every time you listen to music is an opportunity for spirituality. It doesn't matter if you are at home alone, at a concert, in a club, or at a religious service. You listen, you sing along, you get lost, you get absorbed, and you feel fantastic. At the point remember that life is great. It is that easy. Remember that feeling. You can take it with you.

And it is even better if you are a musician (any musician – professional or amateur). Your world is filled with opportunity. Focus every time you practice, rehearse, jam, and perform. Close your eyes. Wow. It is great to be alive. And that awareness is a spiritual experience.

That awareness is the essence of growth as well. Growth is a spiritual term. It means you learned something, changed something, or did something to gain a greater appreciation or understanding of reality. Your faults, challenges, problems, weaknesses, and bad moods are blocks. They blind you to reality. They cause you to react in a stupid or childish way, make bad decisions, and make excuses. They make you self-absorbed. And they make it impossible to be happy.

But when you are aware, when you know that it is great to be alive, when you feel it – you overcome. You shift your perspective from bad to good. You grow. You transcend. And you are one step closer to a better life and a better world.

Music is an opportunity. Spirituality is an opportunity. Don't miss the opportunity. Use it. Use it every day. Reinforce your awareness, flex your spiritual muscles, and be happy. It is the only thing you really want.

# 10
# Music as a Universal Language

The geeky science of music, how you can understand everyone, and the role of spiritual self-expression (Please note: the information at the beginning of this chapter is very technical. If you find it overwhelming, skim until you get to the meaty stuff a few pages in.)

The world is a giant musical instrument. Everything you bang, hit, pluck, blow, or shake makes a sound.

Try it out.

Bang on a piece of wood. Bang on a piece of metal. Bang on your belly. Flick your finger against your taut cheek. Clap your hands. Blow into a tube or over the top of a bottle. Vibrate a reed or a blade of grass with your breath. Press your lips against a metal pipe and blow. Pluck, strike, strum, or bow a string. Sing. Lick your finger and rub the rim of a glass of water. Bang a gong. Anything and everything makes a sound.

Sound is a vibration transmitted through a medium like an elastic solid, liquid, or gas. The vibration is at a frequency that falls within a range that is capable of being detected by the human ear (usually between 20 and

20,000 Hertz or number of beats/vibrations per second).[58] And most things – when you bang, hit, pluck, blow, or shake them – vibrate in a similar way.

The tone – or primary sound you hear – is called a pitch. You can often identify the pitch and notate it within a musical system (although it may fall between the cracks). And that is true whether the sound is a car horn, the Doppler effect of a passing siren, an elephant, fingernails on a blackboard, a tuba, a clap of thunder, or the *Alphabet Song* sung by your tone-deaf kindergarten teacher.

And you don't just hear a single pitch. You hear a combination of pitches. The primary pitch is called the fundamental. It is the pitch you identify, try to notate, and would sing back if asked to produce or match that sound. The other pitches are called overtones.

The fundamental is the primary or dominant sound you hear. It also has the slowest number of vibrations per second (in other words, it is the lowest frequency). The overtones are secondary and vibrate at a faster rate based on subdivisions of the fundamental's frequency. The pattern of subdivisions is a predictable and regular pattern – it happens the same way every time – and it is called the overtone series.[59] Although these secondary vibrations produce distinct and identifiable sounds, your ear fuses them together. Instead of separate harmonics or related frequency components, you hear an identifiable tone that has a distinct timbre (or tone color).[60] Any tone possesses all the notes in its harmonic series to varying degrees, and that variability is the reason why an oboe doesn't sound like a trumpet, even when playing the same note. Their harmonics have different strengths; you just hear them fused together as a single pitch.[61]

You are accustomed to hearing a fusion of overtones. It is the normal way you hear. It is so normal that if you were to remove the fundamental and only play the overtones, you would still hear the fundamental anyway.[62] Small stereo speakers produce bass sounds using this effect.[63] It is like an audio optical illusion.

Not everything produces harmonic overtones (whole number ratios in relation to the fundamental). Sometimes the overtones are inharmonic.[64] That is the reason cymbals, gongs, and trucks crashing into walls sound the way they do. And scientists have produced pure tones – tones without overtones – but those tones are bland and boring. The world is filled with sounds and those sounds are a potpourri of fundamentals, overtones, vibrations, and wild combinations.

Beautiful. And it isn't a new idea. Some people ascribe it to Pythagoras. That may or may not be true. But the idea – as proven when you experiment with a monochord – is an old one.

You probably did the monochord experiment in your high school physics class. Take a string. Stretch it across two fixed points. Pluck it. Put your finger in the exact middle. And your finger creates a harmonic.[65] That means that if the string vibrated at 100 beats per second, after you put your finger in the middle, the two halves of the string vibrated at 200 beats per second. That doubling is the first overtone in the overtone series. That new pitch – in relation to the first – is called an octave in western music. And you can do the experiment at different ratios, too. Divide the monochord into thirds, fourths, *ad infinitum* to find different overtones from the overtone series.

The types of harmonics produced in the monochord experiment are sounds you hear all the time. It is the famous guitar introduction to *Roundabout*, the song by the rock band Yes. It is the way *Portrait of Tracy* – Jaco Pastorius's solo bass piece – is played.

And the effect isn't limited to strings. It happens with metal and wood as well. If you bang on a piece of metal or wood – like a xylophone or marimba – the struck object creates overtones just like a vibrating string does. If you blow a column of air through a metal or wooden tube, the sound you produce has overtones as well. It is the science behind brass instruments. You produce higher or lower notes by loosening or tightening your lips. Your lips find and play the overtones that naturally exist in the metal.

It is also one of the ways a skilled woodwind player can manipulate the reed.[66] I once saw master soprano saxophonist Steve Lacy play full scales without moving his fingers. He did it by playing the reed's harmonics. It was incredible to watch.

But there is more. The overtones vibrate at simple ratios to the fundamental and the sequence is not random. The sequence is always an octave (2:1), fifth (3:2), fourth (4:3), major third (5:4), minor third (6:5), two intervals that fall between a minor third and a whole tone (7:6 and 8:7), and so on at progressively smaller intervals. It is thought that the prevalence of the octave, fifth, fourth, and major and minor thirds in the lower part of the harmonic series contributed to the development of western harmony, in which those intervals form the most common components of chords.[67]

Organizing these sounds – both harmonic and inharmonic – is the way you create music. Melody is the liner organization of sounds, i.e. one pitch after another. Harmony is the organization of multiple pitches simultaneously. Rhythm is how you organize the pulse or motion of sound. I can go on.

But the organizational system you choose is subjective. It is relative to your culture, the part of the world you live in, the tools and technologies you have at your disposal, your age, your generation, the time period you live in, and even your religious beliefs. It is also a question of taste, personality, creativity, intelligence, and your emotional state at the time. Music is personal.

Organizational systems are not just subjective. They often don't work. The history of western tuning is a classic example. Developments in music were not in sync with the realities of the harmonic series in nature.

For example, look at the circle of fifths. Pick a note. Play a note a fifth higher – i.e. an interval that naturally vibrates at a 3:2 ratio in relation to the first note. And do that again twelve times. After twelve notes you arrive back at the original note. It creates a circle (and hence the name). It is a cool phenomenon. Some people think it has spiritual significance. And it plays a big role in contemporary jazz and classical theory. John Coltrane painted the circle of fifths on his wall.[68] He looked at it when he practiced. *Giant Steps*, his famous – and impossible – classic is based on a triangle drawn on the circle of fifths.

Cool stuff. Except that it doesn't work. Stack fifths at an acoustically pure ratio of 3:2 and do the math. Twelve notes later – the note that is supposed to close the circle overshoots the mark by about a quarter step.[69] That is not just out of tune. That is a completely different note. Oops.

Musicians, instrument manufacturers, and educated listeners were aware of that problem for hundreds of years. The solution – one that closed the circle of fifths and allowed musicians to play in tune in any key – was equal temperament. Equal temperament is the standard tuning system used in western music today. It is a system that divides an octave into twelve equal parts: the intervals are out of tune when compared to the simple ratios that occur in nature, but it works. It has been the standard in the west for about one hundred years. You are used to it. It sounds good. But it is a subjective, cultural solution to a real world problem.

Other cultures divide the octave in ways that differ from the west. Some use more than twelve notes. Some use less. Most contain notes not found in the classical western system. (The famous blue note heard in jazz, the blues, and most pop music is not part of a twelve-note system. You won't find it on your piano.) Some systems seem out of tune to western ears. But you can use them and create great music.

And these distinctions don't just apply to melody and harmony. Compare the rhythmic complexity of the music of West Africa or Southern India to the simple rhythms of the west. The systems are completely different. And the difference is not just in complexity – the relationship and understanding of time and its subdivisions is different as well. In some systems, the western concept of meter doesn't even apply.[70]

But there is more. These distinctions are not limited to large groups like countries, cultures, regions, religions, and time periods; they vary from person to person as well. Think about it. The way you speak is unique. Your voice, vocal quality, syntax, phrasing, slang, expressions, thought process, analogies you choose, and even your perspective are unique to you. Nobody speaks the way you do – they may share the same language – but they do not share your voice.

The way you organize sound into music is similar. You share a language – a way of understanding music – with your society. You speak the same language as your peers. But the way you make music is unique. No one sounds like you.

But – and this is the point – it doesn't matter. That is the magic of music. Your music is personal and individual, yet I understand you. It doesn't matter that I come from a different country, era, generation, religion, culture, or planet. I do not need to be familiar with your system, harmony, rhythm, or how you divide the octave. I don't need to know your scales. I don't need to understand your instruments or technology. I understand you. We communicate. I feel your pain, cry, laugh, or share your joy. We bond. You touch my soul. We share a moment. And we become friends. We come from different places. We believe different things. We don't speak the same language. But it doesn't matter. Music transcends those things. We communicate.

Spoken language is limited. You need a shared vocabulary and context to communicate. Music transcends those limitations. You just need to listen.

The universality of music is a spiritual idea. It is in the Bible. Check out the story of the Tower of Babel from the Book of Genesis. In the story, humanity built a tower and rebelled against God. They spoke a common language – communication was universal – and they declared spiritual holy war. But God thwarted their plans. He confused language, made communication impossible, and ended universal communication.[71]

Except for music.

Music is a remnant from the old world. It is a taste of universal communication. It is a reminder that we can understand each other.[72] We have different beliefs. We come from different places. We say things differently. But we have more similarities than differences. We can communicate. Music is the language. I speak it. You hear it. Listen and understand me. We can get along.

God created an amazing world. It is filled with beautiful things. It is inspiring and incredible. But it isn't perfect. It is a world of troubles, problems, challenges, and imperfections. And the imperfections are by design.

Music is an example of that. It isn't perfect – I listed some of the problems above. It needs to be tweaked. How you tweak it is up to you. But once you use it, fix it, and create something; you communicate. You communicate with other people. You can even communicate with God.

The message is obvious: God gave you tools. He gave you music. He gave you the ability to create a dialogue. He gave you the tools to identify and understand something about everyone. And most importantly, He gave you the ability to communicate and establish a relationship with Him.

But the ball is in your court. You have the tools at your disposal. The relationship is up to you. It is there if you want it.

Do you want it?

# Endnotes

1 *Mingus: A critical biography*, Brian Priestly, Da Capo Press, New York, 1982, page 192

2 The term LVS was coined by guitarist Keith Richards and refers to the over-inflated ego common to most lead vocalists. From Keith Richards' book, *Life*, Keith Richards with James Fox, Little, Brown and Company, New York, 2010, page 454

3 *The Real Frank Zappa Book*, Frank Zappa with Peter Occhiogrosso, Touchtone/Simon & Schuster, 1989, Page 185 (emphasis in original quote)

4 Vocal versus instrumental music is discussed in the Talmud in the section Arachin, page 11A. Specifically, the Talmud is trying to ascertain if the essence of song is vocal – and the instruments are merely in the background – or if the instruments play an essential role as well.

5 *Musicophilia: Tales of Music and the Brain*, Oliver Sacks, Alfred A. Knopf Publishing, New York, 2007, Page 239

6 *I am Ozzy*, Ozzy Osbourne with Chris Ayres, Grand Central Publishing, New York, 2009, Page 168

7 Genesis 2:7 based on Rashi and Onkelos. I am using the Artscroll Stone Edition Chumash and borrowing from their commentary as well. Mesorah Publication, Brooklyn NY, 1993

8 I remember seeing a movie AC/DC made of one of their concerts. It was awesome.

9 *The Effects of Music on Memory*, Sara B. Kirkweg, Department of Psychology, Missouri Western State University, 2009: http://clearinghouse.missouriwestern.edu/manuscripts/230.php

10 Also see this: There is also emerging evidence in support of using song to motivate student learning. For example, VanVoorhis (2002) conducted a study on two sections of (psychology) statistics students of equal GPA's. One section read 3 definitions in prose form, and the other sang jingle versions of the definitions. The singing section performed significantly better ($t69 = 2.01, p < .05$) on a set of four short-answer test items. That section had a significant correlation ($r31 = .37, p = .04$) between performance and student self-rating on familiarity with the jingle. The effectiveness of songs has recently been increasingly researched in other fields, such as Crowther (2006) and McCurdy et al. (2008).

Berk, R. A. (2001), "Using Music with Demonstrations to Trigger Laughter and Facilitate Learning in Multiple Intelligences," Journal on Excellence in College Teaching, 12(1), 87-107.

Crowther, G. (2006), "Learning to the Beat of a Different Drum," Connect, 19(4), 11-13.

McCurdy, S. M., Schmiege, C., and Winter, C. K. (2008), "Incorporation of Music in a Food Service Food Safety Curriculum for High School Students," Food Protection Trends, 28(2), 107-114.

VanVoorhis, C.R.W. (2002), "Stat Jingles: To Sing or Not to Sing," Teaching of Psychology, 29(3), 249-250.

Larry Lesser & Dennis Pearl (2008). "Functional Fun in Statistics Teaching: Resources, Research, and Recommendations." Journal of Statistics Education, 16(3), 1-11. http://www.amstat.org/publications/jse/v16n3/lesser.pdf

11 *Shoe History: The History of Your Shoes*, I found it online, the article only noted the following as its source: "'How

American Shoes are Made' with the permission of United Shoe Machinery Corporation": http://www.shoeinfonet.com/about%20shoes/history/history%20your%20shoes/history%20your%20shoes.htm | Shoes found in Oregon: http://pages.uoregon.edu/connolly/FRsandals.htm

12 Exodus 3:5 "Do not come any closer. Take your shoes off your feet."

13 Deuteronomy 25:5-10

14 Ruth 3:7 Ruth uncovered Boaz's feet (he was sleeping at the time) to indicate that he was not wearing shoes. This was a hint to him suggesting that he needed to perform a Levirate Marriage with her.

15 Technically Jews only don't wear leather shoes on Yom Kippur. But the concept is the same: you have to step out of your body – or at least not get distracted – to be spiritual.

16 *Church Turned Club Is Now a Market*, C. J. Hughes, The New York Times, March 16, 2010: http://www.nytimes.com/2010/03/17/realestate/commercial/17limelight.html

17 *Strange Things Happen: A Life with the Police, Polo, and Pygmies*, Stewart Copeland, Harper Collins, New York, 2009, Pages 259-262

18 This section is taken from my book, *Everything You Want Is Really Jewish*, Mekabel Press, 2009, pages 39-40

19 You probably noticed that I took these categories from the Meyers-Briggs personality system. The best book on the subject is *Please Understand Me II* by David Keirsey. I am not a psychologist and I am not endorsing this system over any other. I chose this system as an example because it is clear and easy to articulate. In my opinion, whatever system you choose is immaterial. The important thing is that you choose a system – if you need one – and take time to understand who you are.

20 This is the *Secret of Happiness* by Rabbi Noah Weinberg *ztz'l*, you can find his article here: http://www.aish.com/sp/f/48968901.html

21 I didn't know that either. I looked it up.

22 *How much alcohol is too much at outdoor concerts?* Steve Barnes, Times Union, June 13, 2010: http://www.timesunion.com/news/article/How-much-alcohol-is-too-much-at-outdoor-concerts-559278.php

23 I should note – I am not asking why musicians get stoned – that is a different question. Just why do people use drugs when they listen to music?

24 I found this interview and quote online, there is a lot more in his books as well. This article is a good start however: *William Burroughs: A Sketch*, Citation: Kramer JC. "William Burroughs: A Sketch." Journal of Psychoactive Drugs. Jan-Mar 1981; 13(1): 95-97: http://www.erowid.org/culture/characters/burroughs_william/burroughs_william_article1.shtml Interviewer: "Has anything useful come to you with mescaline or psilocybin?" Burroughs: "Yes, but mostly of an unpleasant nature. There is one interesting one though, yagé, but I've never been able to get any since I left South America. There's Banisteriopsis in it; that's the main ingredient but not the only one. The medicine men use it to potentiate their powers, to locate lost objects and that kind of thing. But I'm not impressed much by their performance. Everybody has telepathic experiences all the time. These things are not rare. It's just an integral part of life. The faculty is probably increased to some extent by any consciousness expanding drug."

25 http://www.catholic.com/library/Who_Can_Receive_Communion.asp

You must believe in the doctrine of transubstantiation. "For anyone who eats and drinks without discerning the body eats and drinks judgment upon himself" (1 Cor. 11:29). Transubstantiation means more than the Real Presence. According to transubstantiation, the bread and wine are actually transformed into the actual body, blood, soul, and divinity of Christ, with only the appearances of bread and wine remaining. This is why, at the Last Supper,

Jesus held what *appeared* to be bread and wine, yet said: "This *is* my body. . . . This *is* my blood" (Mark 14:22-24, cf. Luke 22:14-20). If Christ were merely present along side bread and wine, he would have said "This *contains* my body. . . . This *contains* my blood," which he did not say.

26 Schaffer Library of Drug Policy, *Indian Hemp Drugs Commission Report*, Chapter IX, Social and Religious Customs: http://www.druglibrary.net/schaffer/Library/studies/inhemp/4chapt9.htm (Check the site for list of commission members and principle authors): 435. It is chiefly in connection with the worship of Siva, the Mahadeo or great god of the Hindu trinity, that the hemp plant, and more especially perhaps ganja, is associated. The hemp plant is popularly believed to have been a great favourite of Siva, and there is a great deal of evidence before the Commission to show that the drug in some form or other is now extensively used in the exercise of the religious practices connected with this form of worship. Reference to the almost universal use of hemp drugs by fakirs, jogis, sanyasis, and ascetics of all classes, and more particularly of those devoted to the worship of Siva, will be found in the paragraphs of this report dealing with the classes of the people who consume the drugs. These religious ascetics, who are regarded with great veneration by the people at large, believe that the hemp plant is a special attribute of the god Siva, and this belief is largely shared by the people. Hence the of many fond epithets ascribing to ganja the significance of a divine pro-party, and the common practice of invoking the deity in terms of adoration before placing the chillum or pipe of ganja to the lips. There is evidence to show that on almost all occasions of the worship of this god, the hemp drugs in some form or other are used by certain classes of the people it is established by the evidence of Mahamabopadhya Mahesa Chandra Nyayaratna and of other witnesses that siddhi is offered to the image of Siva at Benares, Baldynath, Tarakeswar, and elsewhere. At the Shivratri festival, and on almost all occasions before the on

which this worship is practised, there is abundant evidence Commission which shows not only that ganja is offered to the god and consumed by these classes of the worshippers, but that these customs are so intimately connected with their worship that they may be considered to form in some sense an integral part of it.

Also see this: *Marijuana - The First Twelve Thousand Years*: http://www.druglibrary.org/schaffer/hemp/history/first12000/1.htm

(Please note that these articles are linked to a site that is in favor of legalizing drugs. Take these sources with a grain of salt.)

27 Specifically, the lines are blurred to the point that you can no longer distinguish between "cursed is Haman and blessed is Mordechai."

28 Purim is the only time a person is supposed to drink a lot. Judaism does not encourage excessive drinking or drunkenness. If you disagree, check out the Talmud in Sanhedrin: The rabbis ask, "Why does drunkenness feel the way it does?" And they answer, "In order to give the wicked their reward in this world and not the next."

29 Check out this video explaining datura and the connection to God: http://www.youtube.com/watch?v=zEUG9jdFJFI - Also note that datura is extremely dangerous.

30 *Sufi tokers and the green saint*, Chris Bennet, April 13 2001, Cannabis Culture Magazine: http://www.cannabisculture.com/articles/1883.html (You should probably take this and the previous note with a grain of salt as well.)

31 This is from "Houses of the Holy" by Led Zeppelin. I know it is really cheesy to quote song lyrics like this. But I couldn't resist.

32 Lots of people quote this Chinese saying in articles online, but the only source I could find was Wikipedia! I am sorry if it is only an urban legend: http://en.wikipedia.org/wiki/In_vino_veritas

33 Is this a scientific fact? I don't know. Go here to see some of the debate after Mel Gibson's infamous anti-Semitic drunken rant: *Is Alcohol A Truth Serum? Doctors Ponder The Effects Of Booze In The Wake Of Mel Gibson's Tirade*, Sean Alfano, CBSNews.com, Aug. 3, 2006: http://www.cbsnews.com/stories/2006/08/03/health/webmd/main1864620.shtml

34 Rabbi Noah Weinberg *ztz'l* said this all the time.

35 *Genius*, James Gleick, Pantheon Books, New York, 1992, page 397

36 Judges 9:13. The exact quote is, "But the vine said to them, 'Shall I give up my wine that gladdens God and man?'"

37 Babylonian Talmud, *Arachin*, Page 11A

38 "[The] emotional response to groove occurs via the ear-cerebellum-nucleus accumbens-limbic circuit rather than via the ear-auditory cortex circuit. Our response to groove is largely pre- or unconscious because it goes through the cerebellum rather than the frontal lobes. What is remarkable is that all of these different pathways integrate into our experience of a single song." *This is Your Brain on Music: the science of a human obsession*, Daniel J. Levitin, Penguin Group, New York, 2006, page 192.

39 I am not using the dictionary definitions of intellect and intuition here. These are spiritual terms. My understanding of these terms is based on Rashi's comments on Deuteronomy 1:13 (based on the Midrash). "The wise man is similar to a rich moneychanger. When someone brings him money to look at, he looks at it. When no one brings him money, he sits and doesn't do anything. The man of understanding is similar to a moneychanger who shows initiative. When someone brings him money to look at, he looks at it. When no one brings him money, he goes out and drums up business." In this analogy, the wise man is a euphonium for wisdom or the intellect (*chochmah* in Hebrew). The man of understanding is a euphonium for understanding or intuition (*bina* in Hebrew). In other

words, the intellect is information-based but superficial and lacking depth. Intuition implies a deeper understanding. It takes effort to comprehend and transcends the intellect.

40 This concept of mood is found in the Bible in Proverbs 12:25. "Worry in a man's heart will bring him down, a good thing will make him happy." Rabbi Meir Leib Weiser, better known as the Malbim (the great 19th Century commentator), retranslates this verse – based on a careful reading of the Hebrew – like this: "When a person is worried he should either suppress the worry or enjoy something good." In other words, the good thing will distract him from worry and change his mood for the better.

41 The tritone is a musical interval three whole steps from the tonic. Jazz musicians call it the flat fifth. Others call it an augmented fourth. It is the opening interval in the song "Black Sabbath" by the band Black Sabbath. It also precedes the main riff to "Purple Haze" by Jimi Hendrix.

42 I know, another song reference. I can't help myself. This is from "Tomorrow Never Knows" by the Beatles. But you probably know that already.

43 *Life*, Keith Richards with James Fox, Little, Brown and Company, New York, 2010, page 454

44 *Miles, the autobiography*, Miles Davis with Quincy Troupe, Simon and Schuster, New York, 1989, page 199 (emphasis in the original)

45 The source is the *Code of Jewish Law* or *Shulchan Aruch* O.C. 5. "When a person mentions the name of God, he should a) concentrate on the explanation of the name he says and understand that God is the 'Master of All Reality.' And b) he should concentrate on the written form of the name and understand that God 'is, was, and always will be.' When he mentions the 'Elokim' name of God he should understand that God is 'All-Able and All-Powerful.'" The *Mishna Berurah* quotes the Vilna Goan (the great Rabbi Eliyahu from Vilna)(M.B. 5:3) and explains further, "[A person] doesn't need to have this focus every time he mentions the

name of God, except when reading the Shema (the Shema is the primary declaration of faith in Judaism)…" The point here is that when you say the Shema you have to think that God is: a) Master of all reality, b) is, was, and always will be, and c) all-powerful. The first verse of Shema concludes, "God is one." In other words, God is the only reality, the only reality not bound by time, and the only power – or more simply – the unlimited source of existence.

46 Technically speaking, you can't define God as *anything*. Rabbi Moshe Chaim Luzzatto makes this point over and over again in the *Da'as T'vunos*. As my teacher, Rabbi Yochanan Bechhofer explained Rabbi Luzzatto, "You can't know what God is. You can only know what God does. And really you can't even know that – you can only know the *results* of what He did." Based on this understanding it is only correct (at most) to call God "the source of reality." However, for the sake of simplicity – and particularly since this is how man relates to Him – I chose here to refer to God as "reality." My Rosh Yeshiva, Rabbi Noah Weinberg *ztz'l* often referred to God simply as "reality" as well.

47 Yes, I know this is an oversimplification.

48 *Meditation and the Bible*, Aryeh Kaplan, Samuel Weisner Inc, York Beach Maine, 1978, page 64

49 *This is Your Brain on Music: the science of a human obsession*, Daniel J. Levitin, Penguin Group, New York, 2006, Page 252

50 *In Search of a Liszt to Be Loved*, Johanna Keller, The New York Times, January 14, 2001: http://www.nytimes.com/2001/01/14/arts/14KELL.html?pagewanted=all

51 *Etymology of Jazz: JAS, JASS, JAZ, JASCZ or just plain JAZZ*, A Passion for Jazz: http://www.apassion4jazz.net/etymology.html

52 *Reagan Proposes School Prayer Amendment*, AP (The New York Times); National Desk, The New York Times, May 18, 1982: http://www.nytimes.com/1982/05/18/us/reagan-proposes-school-prayer-amendment.html

53 http://www.wearegrace.org/9-11_images/wtc-bushpray.jpg

54 Comedian Steve Martin said it best, "When you study philosophy, you learn just enough to screw you up for the rest of your life."

55 This experiment is from my teacher, Rabbi Noah Weinberg *ztz'l*

56 *His Name was Nachshon Wachsman*, Esther Wachsman, May 9, 2000: http://www.ou.org/yerushalayim/yomhazikaron/wachsman.htm

57 Interesting article: *8 lottery winners who lost their millions*, Ellen Goodstein, Bankrate.com, January 2005: http://articles.moneycentral.msn.com/SavingandDebt/SaveMoney/8lotteryWinnersWhoLostTheirMillions.aspx

58 *The American Heritage Dictionary of the English Language, Fourth Edition*, Houghton Mifflin Company, 2000: http://web.archive.org/web/20080625012016/http://www.bartleby.com/61/65/S0576500.html

59 Here is a more technical definition taken from the *Grove Dictionary of Music Online* (author Murray Campbell) "One of the frequency components of a sound other than that of lowest frequency. Usually overtones are numbered consecutively in ascending order of frequency; they need not be harmonic." I found it here: http://www.music.sc.edu/fs/bain/atmi02/hs/index-audio.html

60 Also taken from here: *The Harmonic Series: A path to understanding musical intervals, scales, tuning and timbre*, Reginald Bain, Updated: April 1, 2003: http://www.music.sc.edu/fs/bain/atmi02/hs/index-audio.html - but you can find these same ideas in many sources.

61 *How Equal Temperament Ruined Harmony (and Why You Should Care)*, Ross W. Duffin, W.W. Norton and Co., NY, 2007, Page 21

62 It is called the Restoration of the Missing Fundamental, you can read an interesting study here: *Neuromagnetic Evidence for Early Auditory Restoration of Fundamental Pitch*,

Philip J. Monahan, Kevin de Souza, William J. Idsardi, Published: August 6, 2008: http://www.plosone.org/article/info%3Adoi%2F10.1371%2Fjournal.pone.0002900

63 There are many studies and papers explaining this phenomenon. Here is a link to someone's doctoral thesis on the topic: *Quantifying The Consonance of Complex Tones with Missing Fundamentals*, Song Hui Chon, June 2008: https://ccrma.stanford.edu/~shchon/pubs/shchon-thesis-final.pdf

You can find many other published examples as well

64 An inharmonic overtone is when the frequencies of the overtones are not integer multiples of the fundamental. See here (and to hear a few examples, too): *Handbook for Acoustic Ecology, Second Edition*, Barry Truax, editor (Originally published by the World Soundscape Project, Simon Fraser University, and ARC Publications, 1978), Cambridge Street Publishing, 1999: http://www.sfu.ca/sonic-studio/handbook/Inharmonic.html and also look at the link above in endnote 51.

65 This is the way I remembered doing the monochord experiment in high school. My friend Larry Lesser – a math professor at the University of Texas in El Paso – owns a monochord and noted that my memory is not consistent with how the experiment is actually done. On Larry's monochord, you have a movable bridge placed under the string but between the fixed ends. You change the vibrations/ratios when you use the bridge to divide the string at different points. You can divide it in half, two-thirds/one-third, or however you like.

66 To be more precise, when a guitarist plays a harmonic, he is essentially adjusting the pressure on the string. Reed instruments – like a saxophone – achieve harmonics in a similar way, by increasing pressure on the reed. A saxophone works because the musician blows the fundamental air column and the keys either lengthen or shorten that air column. The second octave is produced with a small vent key that allows you to play the first partial. That key

accomplishes the same effect as applying more pressure on the reed. (Thank you to Binyomin Berke for this explanation and for invaluable assistance understanding this stuff.)

67 *How Equal Temperament Ruined Harmony (and Why You Should Care)*, Ross W. Duffin, W.W. Norton and Co., NY, 2007, Page 21 (paraphrased from the section, "What Is the Harmonic Series?")

68 I don't remember where I heard this, though I believe it was from jazz legend George Russell.

69 *How Equal Temperament Ruined Harmony (and Why You Should Care)*, Ross W. Duffin, W.W. Norton and Co., NY, 2007, Page 25

70 You can find the concept of a moveable one in many different cultures. The most famous example I know of is from Northwest African drumming. Another great example is called a groove canon. The concept and term were coined by drum legend Bob Moses in his incredible book, *Drum Wisdom*.

71 Genesis 11:1-9

72 *Maayan Bies Hashoeva*, Rabbi Shimon Schwab, Mesorah Publications, 1994, Page 20

# Acknowledgements

This book took forever. It started about seventeen years ago when a friend showed me the different discussions about music in the Talmud (the primary sources are in the tractates Arachin and Succos). Someone else told me about *Shir Bina* by Rabbi Shmuel Stern – a wonderful book about music and kaballah (unfortunately it is only available in Hebrew). I was sold. I love music – I played it professionally – and I thought I was the perfect person to write a book about music and spirituality.

But I was busy. The years went by, I wrote other books and did other things. But the music book was in the back of my mind. I started working on it a few times, but something always came up.

I was in Denver this year for Rosh Hashanah. I was staying with friends and talking music nonstop. I was inspired and decided not to do anything else until I wrote the music book. And surprise, I did it. If you like this book, travel to Denver, find the ghost of Jack Kerouac (he is probably still somewhere near Larimer Street), suck up the vibe, and then go to the east side and thank my friends. They will appreciate it.

I want to thank Larry Lesser from the math department at the University of Texas El Paso (and also the mighty El Paso Jewish Community). His enthusiasm for this project is unlimited. He read through the text, found most of the typos, suggested many ways to make the book better, added sources and expertise, and was instrumental in making sure I did a job well done.

I also want to thank Binyomin Berke for his invaluable assistance in completing chapter ten. He went through my first draft, found my mistakes, and added a wealth of information.

I am greatly indebted to my good friends Sarah Liberstein, Avi Glazer, Jason Lombardo, and David Campbell. They read through the manuscript, offered suggestions and guidance, and pushed me to make sure I had it together.

I also owe a huge thank you to my friends Adam Weinberg, Moshe Soloway, Reyna Simnegar, Alexander Seinfeld, David Lieberman, and Adam Jacobs. They each took time – lots of time – from their often hectic schedules to talk to me and explain the big bad world of books, PR, TV, blogs, and the music industry.

I could list every musician who ever influenced me, but that would be lame.

Thank you again to Esther Zaretsky for the wonderful layout and typesetting. This is our fourth book together – it is getting to be a habit. And thank you also to Shira Greenberg for the cool cover.

I owe a massive debt of gratitude to all the amazing people who contributed to make this project a reality. I am so blessed to have so much support from so many great people. You really are the best. I don't want to single anyone out, though I do have to give special mention to my parents. They have been such firm believers in everything I do and their support over the years – all of it and in every way – has been unbelievable. And please mom and dad – don't draw any conclusions from the things I wrote about in chapter four. I really didn't do anything. Really.

And finally – and most of all – I owe a huge thank you to my wife and children. Thank you for supporting all the things I do and being there for me always.

# About the Author

**Tzvi Gluckin** got his first guitar when he was 13. Music was an obsession: he practiced all the time, joined bands, and became a serious rocker. He went to the New England Conservatory of Music in Boston and earned a degree in Jazz Studies. He performed with jazz legends George Russell, Cecil Taylor, and others. Some of his college friends became famous doing the jazz/fussion/mid-90s funk thing. He moved to New York, gigged, taught lessons, toured odd parts of the Midwest, and recorded in a small basement studio in Brooklyn. He was put on the guest list to a P-Funk show at the Ritz in Manhattan and given backstage access. He got to stand next to Bootsy Collins. He was too intimidated to say anything.

But it wasn't enough.

In the summer of 1993, Tzvi bought an open-ended, round trip, good-for-a-year ticket to Europe. He played guitar on the streets (earning about $40 an hour) and became a bohemian. He wandered for six months. He traveled east – always east – played music, and talked deep ideas with anyone who would listen.

His last stop was Israel. He decided to stay for two weeks. But two weeks became four months and four months became seven-and-a-half years. He joined a yeshiva – Aish HaTorah – in Jerusalem's Old City, studied like a manic, analyzed ancient mystical texts, joined the teaching faculty, and earned his rabbinical ordination from Rabbi Noah Weinberg *ztz'l*. He moved to Boston in 2001.

Today Tzvi writes books, records music, travels, lectures, and brags about his beard. He is a very good guitarist. He is not a very good singer. His wife and children complain when he sings at the dinner table. He likes to listen to loud music and he suffers from tinnitus.

You can contact Tzvi via his website at www.gluckin.com.

We are so proud of you
and all of the good you do
at a time when it is
really needed.
Keep up the good work!

Love Mom and Dad

In honor of Aish Boston for their tremendous efforts

From
The Simnegar Family

Hazak u'Baruch to Tzvi Gluckin on yet another tremendous work of Torah!

Dr. and Mrs. Ya'aqob Freedman

For the z'chut of Matityahu ben David and the Memory of Hacham Mordechai Eliyahu zt"l

## Sponsors

Mr. and Mrs. Robert and Joan Gluckin
The Simnegar Family

Dr. and Mrs. Ya'aqob Freedman and Family

SLAM
Rabbi Shlomo and Karen Hochberg
The Klompas Family
Adam Sheps and Rachel Lohr
The Sternberg Family
Joel and Karin Mirkin

## Honor Roll

Amy and Chad Lewis and Family
The Shulman Family
Steven "Koop" Kostick
Mr. and Mrs. Mutty Stein
Sara Weinberg
Alex Rikun
Alina and Zave Monisov

## *Discover This*
### Who Wrote the Torah and How Do You Know?

Can an intelligent, rational, levelheaded, thinking person believe that God wrote the Torah? Good question. *Discover This* is a good answer.

*Discover This* examines the evidence. Specifically it discusses:

- The Contradictory Nature of Jewish Survival
- The Jewish Experience at Mount Sinai
- The Accuracy of the Torah's Transmission
- The Story of the Torah Codes
- The Nazis Hidden in the Book of Esther

And much more

*Discover This* is unleashed, full-throttle, unadulterated, and no-nonsense. It is authoritative, documented, and well researched. It is quality. And it is what you expect, fun to read and easy to understand.

*Discover This*: Read it. Think about it. And decide for yourself.

Get your copy today: www.gluckin.com/book

*Everything You Want Is Really Jewish* is a book about pseudo-hipsters, hairstyles, loud music, Czech beer, shwarma, the art of New York driving, music school, Israel, and the Earth Jew. It is about identity and asking questions. It is about being Jewish. It is about frustration and not knowing what to ask. It is about everything: and that everything you want, you already know.

Get your copy today:
www.gluckin.com/book

## If you liked the book, you will love the talk!

### Bring *Knee Deep in the Funk* to your community today.

Tzvi Gluckin is an engaging, dynamic, hysterical, thought provoking, and veteran speaker. He is available for every type of speaking engagement including weekend retreats, full-day seminars, evening programs, high school events, campus programs, young professional events, singles events, keynote addresses, fundraising events, parlor meetings, training sessions, consulting, and every other event, program, seminar, or thing you can think of!

Tzvi has a full array of programs, talks, seminars, and inspirational speeches to chose from. His prices are affordable, negotiable, include perks, and are geared to fit your budget. Tzvi will go the extra mile to make sure you get an amazing program at a price you can afford.

### Contact Tzvi today and bring him to your town!

For more information and to book online visit www.gluckin.com or email Tzvi directly at tzvi.gluckin@gmail.com.

www.ingramcontent.com/pod-product-compliance
Lightning Source LLC
Chambersburg PA
CBHW032135040426
42449CB00005B/248